Puppet Plays

PUPPET PLAYS
From Workshop to Performance

By Toni A. Schramm

Illustrated by Leann Mullineaux

1993
TEACHER IDEAS PRESS
A Division of
Libraries Unlimited, Inc.
Englewood, Colorado

To Heidi and Holly, my first audience

TEACHER IDEAS PRESS
A Division of
Libraries Unlimited, Inc.
P.O. Box 6633
Englewood, CO 80155-6633

Library of Congress Cataloging-in-Publication Data

Schramm, Toni A.
   Puppet plays : from workshop to performance / by Toni A. Schramm ; illustrated by Leann Mullineaux.
   xii, 194 p. 22x28 cm.
   Includes bibliographical references (p. 189) and index.
   ISBN 1-56308-100-8
   1. Puppet theater. 2. Puppet plays. I. Title.
PN1972.S413 1993
791.5'3--dc20   93-14986
                                                                  CIP

Contents

Acknowledgments

I wish to thank a number of people without whom this book would not have been possible:

- Betsy and Mike Meyer for their computer and for countless hours of help

- Julie Trychta, who encouraged me to begin

- The librarians at the Lake Villa District Library who helped with the early puppet shows, and especially Pat Melcher

- Jim and Sue Magee for the use of their copy machine

- Bonnie and Dan McMenamin and Debby Ply for babysitting and friendship

- My husband, Jim, for his support and ideas

- My editor, Suzanne Barchers, for her help and confidence

- Leann Mullineaux for making my ideas come alive through her illustrations

- Carolyn Pittman for proofreading and suggestions

Introduction

Puppets! Children love them. Many adults enjoy them, too—until called upon to present a puppet show or to teach puppetry to children. Then questions spring up:

- Where can I find puppet shows that will hold the interest of the children?

- Can I teach children to make lasting puppets that are unique, that go beyond the paper bag, paper plate, and sock puppets they made in kindergarten?

- What do I do about scenery, music, and props?

- If I am going to teach puppetry, how do I get organized?

- How can I teach children to put on a performance that doesn't embarrass us all?

Why teach puppetry at all? Why use it in the classroom or have children perform shows at the library or in youth groups? Puppets spark the imagination of children and adults alike. Consider the popularity and endurance of the puppets of Jim Hensen, Fred Rogers, and Shari Lewis. Puppetry is a multisensory means of exploring literature. It can be an interesting way to combine art and language experiences, to provide opportunities for cooperation among children, and to encourage creativity. It may bring shy children out of their shells. Best of all, puppetry is fun.

During my years in the children's department at the Lake Villa District Library in Illinois, I organized performances of puppet shows and ran workshops in which children aged seven through fourteen made puppets and put on shows for audiences of up to 100 children and adults. As a school librarian now, I use puppets in my library and return to the public library each summer to run puppet workshops with children. We've even become a popular entry in the hometown summer parade, waving our puppets to the crowd as we march past with the Friends of the Library.

When I began teaching puppetry, I found very little information about how to proceed and a lack of quality scripts for children. Over the course of several years, I developed my ideas for teaching puppet workshops, and I found I enjoyed writing scripts for puppet shows. This book, developed from my experience, differs from other books about puppetry in that it is directed toward teachers, librarians, and other adults with little or no experience in teaching puppetry. It is for the instructor who wishes to go beyond paper bag puppets to help the children create lasting puppets, each one as unique as the child who made it. The step-by-step instructions and numerous illustrations make this a clear manual for use by an instructor who wishes to teach puppetry to children. The inclusion of chapters about running puppet workshops makes my book unique, as little material is available about teaching puppetry to children.

The book comprises three sections. Part I details puppet making, stages, and scenery. Patterns are provided for making many of the specific puppets needed for performance of the shows included in the book. But part I is not limited to a specific few puppets. Ideas are given for the construction of a wide variety of puppets that you use in shows from other sources or from your imagination. The chapters proceed from the simple stick puppet to more complicated puppets. Ideas are given for stages you may construct and for simple scenery and props children may make.

Part II describes the steps I take in running a puppet workshop. It is a step-by-step procedures manual covering such topics as advance planning, practice exercises with puppets, rehearsal, and performance. It is designed to help you avoid some of the pitfalls of trial and error.

Part III contains eight scripts for puppet shows. These shows are written for children from approximately age four through eleven. All the plays are my original scripts. Three are adaptations of folk or fairy tales. Time constraints often make it difficult for teachers, librarians, and other instructors to write their own scripts or to develop scripts with children. This book provides scripts with interesting characters, action, and suspense. Each script is preceded by notes telling where to find the patterns for making the puppets needed for the show. Where appropriate, notes also refer you to specific scenery details in chapter 4.

The book is intended to be used as a whole. Each section builds upon the previous one. Thus, you begin by learning to construct puppets, scenery, and stages. Then this knowledge is put to use by planning and conducting a puppet workshop. The scripts are provided at the end for you to sample, keeping in mind what has been presented in the first two sections of the book.

Have fun with puppetry. Let your imagination soar as you bring out the creativity in your students. You will be amazed at what they can do, with some guidance from a well-prepared instructor. The children will be proud of the puppets they have made and the performance they have given. The magic of puppetry will come alive, and the children will be asking for more!

Part I
Puppet Construction, Stages, and Scenery

Something magical happens when a puppet speaks and moves. A character comes to life, to the delight of the children — and adults — who listen and watch.

Many elements combine to produce a puppet show. A well-written script, the stage, interesting scenery and music, and skilled puppeteers all contribute to the effectiveness of the show. But the focal point of the production is the puppets themselves. Part I of this book begins with the construction of hand puppets. The chapters proceed from simple stick puppets and easy-to-make felt hand puppets to more complicated Styrofoam™-head puppets. Step-by-step instructions, materials, lists, and patterns are provided for the puppets used in five of the puppet plays included in part III. Suggestions are provided for making additional puppets to use in the other puppet shows.

Because this book is directed toward adults working with children in a workshop setting, the individual differences and abilities of the children need to be kept in mind. The puppets detailed in chapters 1 and 2 may be made entirely by the children with some guidance from the instructor. With the more complicated puppets, or in situations where time is limited, the instructor may wish to prepare the basic body and head forms in advance and allow the children to complete the costumes and faces. Older children and teenagers will be able to follow the instructions provided in chapter 3. An instructor working with younger children (under age eleven or twelve) will be better off beginning with felt or stick puppets.

Whether one sticks to the easier patterns or tackles the more involved ones, this should be remembered: The patterns are included as suggestions and ideas, to provide a spark for the imaginations of the puppet makers; the children should be allowed and encouraged to be creative with the costume designs and facial features. A variety of fabrics (including felts), ribbons, and trims should be provided from which the children may select bits and pieces for their puppets. This is a time to experiment with colors, textures, shapes, and designs. The results will be puppets as unique as the children who make them.

The scenery suggestions are just suggestions. The type of scenery one uses will be determined in part by the type of stage available. Information about stages, scenery, and props completes part I. With a sturdy stage, simple and imaginative scenery, and puppets made with care, the stage is set and the magic can begin.

1

1

Stick Puppets

Puppets come in a broad range of types. They vary from simple paper finger puppets to elaborate marionettes. Puppet show directors must base their choice of puppet type on several factors. If the children will make the puppets as a workshop activity, the amount of time available for puppet making, as well as the ages and abilities of the children, must be considered. The type and size of stage to be used may be a factor. In addition, the type of characters called for in the script may determine the type of puppet to be used.

ADVANTAGES OF STICK PUPPETS

"Star Light, Star Bright," included in part III of this book, is an example of a script for which stick puppets present an answer to the question of how one makes puppets to represent inanimate objects. While not impossible, it is difficult to imagine stars and clouds in the form of hand puppets. Stick puppets, however, lend themselves well to the representation of inanimate objects. They are a good starting point for the beginning puppeteer, as they are simple to make and easy to manipulate.

"Star Light, Star Bright," has been presented with a combination of stick puppets made of felt and felt hand puppets. The inanimate objects—Star Bright, Big Star, and Gray Cloud—were represented by stick puppets (figure 1.1). The lion, mouse, reindeer, and Wendy took the form of simple felt hand puppets. Details for the construction of the latter four puppets are provided in chapter 2, "Felt Hand Puppets." Using hand puppets for these characters allowed the puppeteers to make their puppets wave, tug, and cover their faces with their hands. The use of puppets on sticks for the stars and cloud allowed these characters to "hang" in the sky and allowed Gray Cloud to hover over the other characters.

Fig. 1.1. Big Star, Star Bright, and Gray Cloud from "Star Light, Star Bright."

CONSTRUCTION OF STICK PUPPETS

A stick puppet is made by attaching a puppet face or body to a stick or rod handle. Stick puppets may be constructed from a variety of materials, including felt, cardboard, or even paper plates. The sticks may be made from wood, metal, plastic, or everyday items such as tongue depressors and plastic drinking straws. The puppets may be attached to the sticks with staples, glue, or tape.

Each stick puppet used in "Star Light, Star Bright" is made from two pieces of felt sewn together and stuffed with polyester batting. The handles are made from ⅜-inch dowel rods, available in many hardware stores. Star Bright, Big Star, and Gray Cloud are all constructed in the same general manner. Specific pattern pieces are provided for each puppet following the instructions.

Materials Needed per Puppet

Two 9-by-11½-inch pieces of felt (yellow or gold for stars; gray for cloud)
Extra pieces of felt for eyes, mouth, bows, and lightning bolt (suggested colors: green, blue, pink, red, orange, and yellow)
Fabric craft glue (a long-lasting brand is Tacky Glue™)
Polyester batting (four thicknesses of batting cut into 9-by-11½-inch rectangles)
Thread to match or contrast with felt bodies
Assorted trim, optional (for example, lace for Star Bright's hair bow, sequins for pupils of eyes, glitter for tips of stars)
⅜-inch diameter dowel rod, sanded and cut to 18-inch length
Black paint
Sewing machine
Sharp scissors
Heavy-duty stapler

Method of Construction

Body. Trace the puppet body pattern onto paper and pin onto one of the felt rectangles. With sharp scissors, cut out puppet. Repeat with the second felt rectangle, taking care in cutting so that the two pieces will match exactly.

Trace pattern pieces for facial features and accessories onto the other felt pieces, and carefully cut these out. Place facial features onto one of the body pieces, being sure the eyes are not too high on the face (figure 1.2). This is a common mistake children—and adults—may make in constructing puppets. Do not glue on accessories such as bows or lightning bolt until the two body pieces are sewn together. Adjust placement and then glue facial features onto the body with fabric craft glue. Tacky Glue holds well, and its thick consistency is neater for children to use than white school glue. Tacky Glue is available in craft and fabric stores. Allow glue to dry before proceeding to the next step.

Cut out four thicknesses of batting, using the puppet body pattern. Place plain puppet body (the puppet's back) on the work surface, and then place all four layers of batting on top. Finally, place the puppet body with facial features facing up on top of the batting (figure 1.3). Using a zigzag stitch, sew all thicknesses together with the sewing machine, close to the edge of the body. Be sure to leave approximately ½ inch open at the bottom for insertion of the dowel rod. The thread used in sewing the puppet together may

Fig. 1.2. Placement of facial features.

Big Star   Star Bright   Gray Cloud

Fig. 1.3. Four layers of batting are placed
between the felt body pieces.

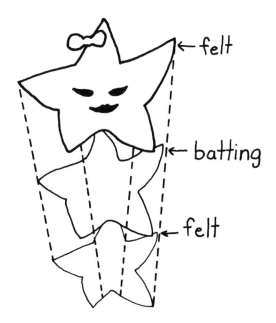

match the felt. Sometimes, however, a contrasting color may add interest or meaning to the character. For example, Gray Cloud's black stitching adds to the sinister appearance—it's the opposite of a "silver lining."

After stitching the puppet together, trim away any batting that may protrude from the front and back of the puppet.

Trim. Determine placement of accessories, referring to figure 1.1. Glue these pieces onto the puppet. Additional trim may be applied at this point. Sequins may accent the eyes, and glitter may be sprinkled over the tips of the stars or onto the lightning bolt.

Handle. If the stage to be used has a black background curtain, the dowel rod should be painted black to be less noticeable. The painting of the rod may be done any time prior to the next step. Four to 5 inches on one end of the rod need not be painted, as this section is inserted inside the puppet. Insert the rod into the puppet through the opening left at the bottom. Staple the felt onto the rod with one or two staples on the front and the back of the puppet.

Figures 1.4 through 1.9 (pages 7 to 14) provide patterns for the star and cloud puppets.

MANIPULATION OF STICK PUPPETS

Stick puppets are simple to operate. The puppeteer grasps the stick near the bottom, keeping her or his hand below the front curtain or wall of the stage, out of sight of the audience (figure 1.10, page 15).

Because stick puppets have no movable mouths or arms, it is essential that the puppet operator move the puppet while that character speaks. If the puppets are not given movement, they will appear to be merely part of the scenery, and the audience will become confused about which character is speaking. (And a confused audience will soon become a restless, noisy audience!) One puppet may turn toward another as it speaks. "Yes" and "no" may be indicated: yes, by moving the puppet's entire body up and down; no, by rotating it from side to side (figure 1.11, page 15). A stick puppet may convey surprise by suddenly stopping a movement, by jumping backwards, or by turning very slowly (as in disbelief) toward another puppet. Practice exercises for puppet movement are supplied in part II.

Stick puppets, then, provide a workshop leader with many advantages. They are easy to construct and to manipulate. They may be used by puppeteers with any size hand; one need not worry about a too-big puppet flopping from a small child's hand or a large hand squeezing into a tiny puppet. And perhaps the greatest advantage of using stick puppets is the ability to represent inanimate objects in a puppet show. Stick puppets may be used in shows that require toys or flowers to come to life. Vehicles such as trains may be represented. "The Little Engine That Could" is an example of a story that may be brought to life with stick puppets.

When designing one's own stick puppets, a puppet maker need not worry about creating a perfect pattern. A star with points of varying lengths can be more interesting to watch than a star with five symmetrical points. Star Bright has a point that curves upward, giving her the appearance of offering a friendly wave. Puppet makers should consider the traits of the characters in the script. Then their imagination may create unique puppets with facial features, trim, and accessories that emphasize friendliness, hostility, beauty, or timidity. A stick puppet, then, is simple to make but, with some understanding of the character by the maker, may convey a personality that matches its actions and words.

Fig. 1.4. Pattern for Star Bright body (continued on page 8).

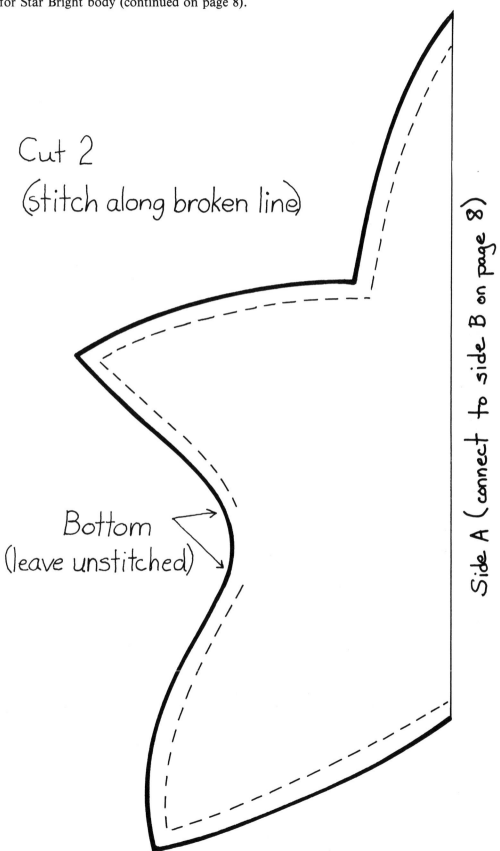

Cut 2
(stitch along broken line)

Bottom
(leave unstitched)

Side A (connect to side B on page 8)

Fig. 1.4.

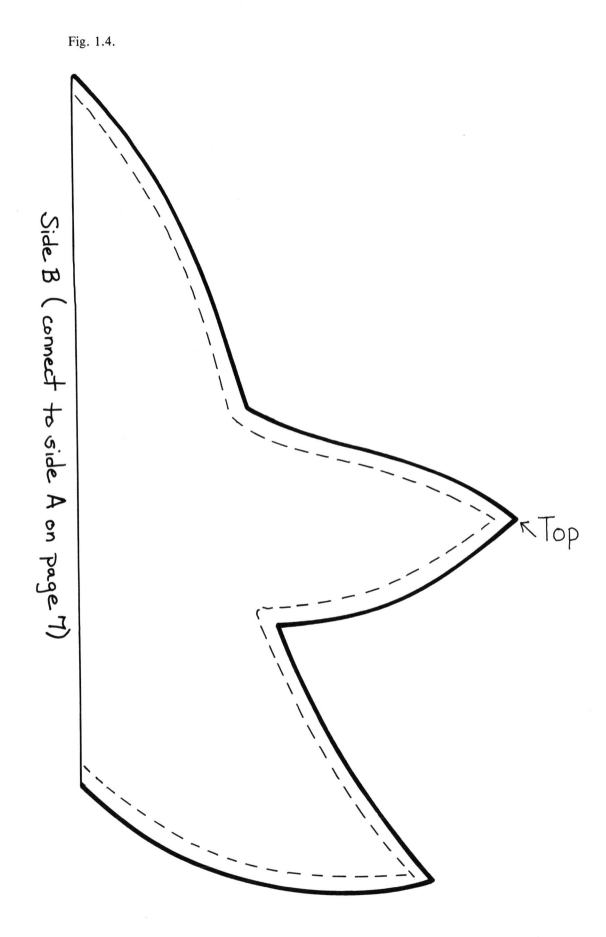

Side B (connect to side A on page 7)

←Top

Fig. 1.5. Pattern for Big Star body (continued on page 10).

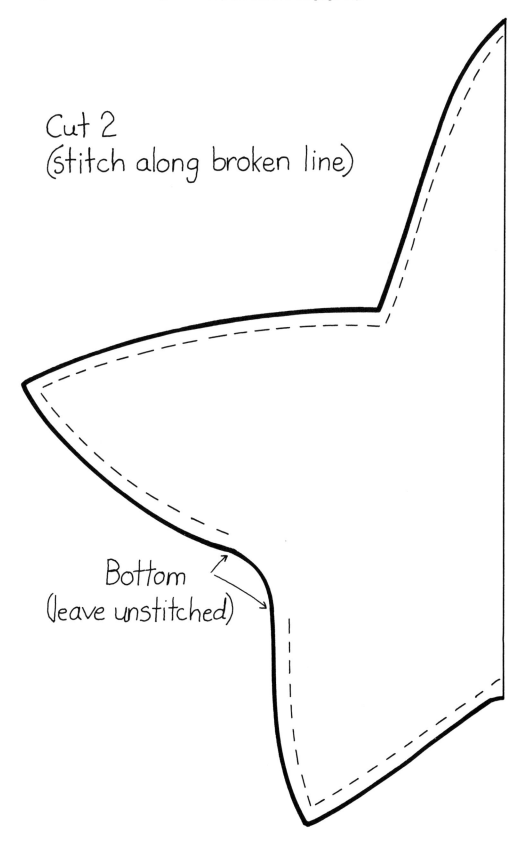

Cut 2
(stitch along broken line)

Bottom
(leave unstitched)

Fig. 1.5.

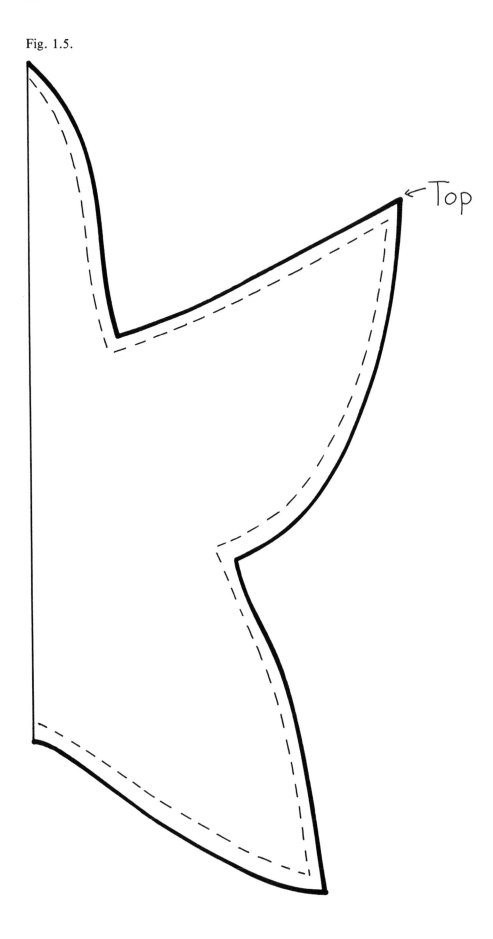

Fig. 1.6. Pattern for Gray Cloud body (continued on page 12).

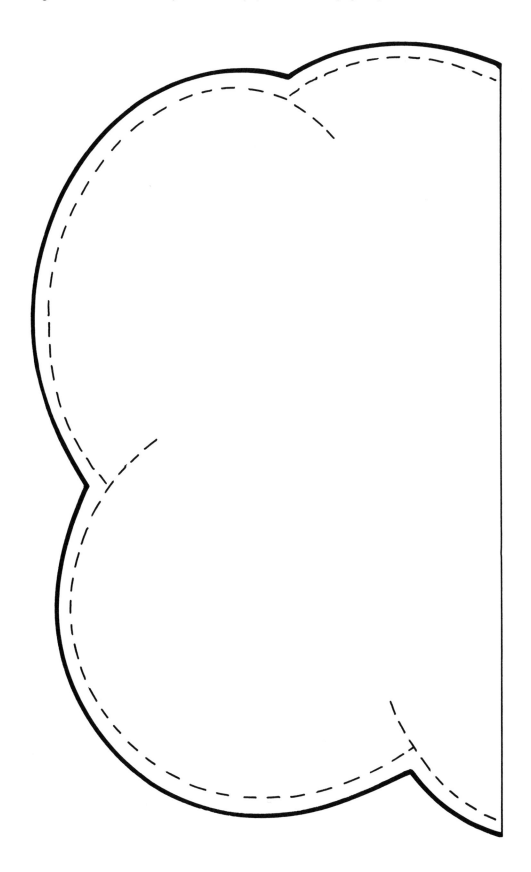

Fig. 1.6.

Cut 2 (Stitch along broken line)

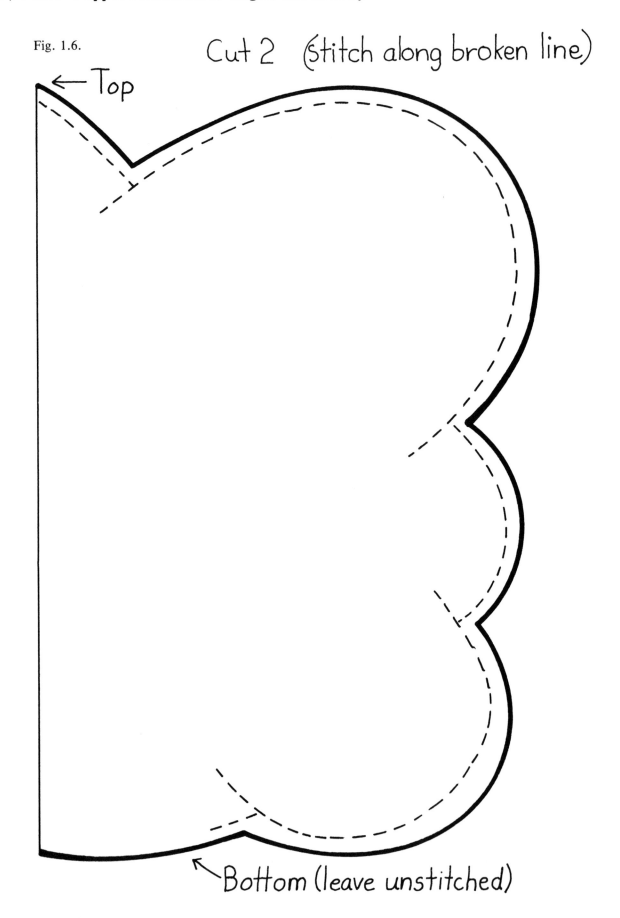

← Top

↖ Bottom (leave unstitched)

Fig. 1.7. Patterns for Star Bright.

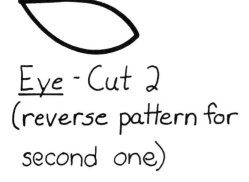

Eye - Cut 2
(reverse pattern for
second one)

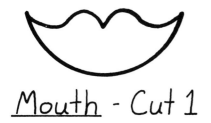

Mouth - Cut 1

Hair bow - Cut 1

Fig 1.8. Patterns for Big Star.

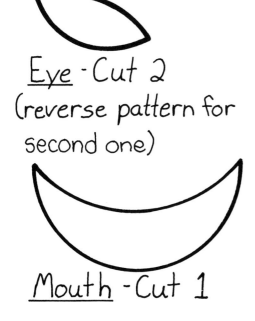

Eye - Cut 2
(reverse pattern for
second one)

Mouth - Cut 1

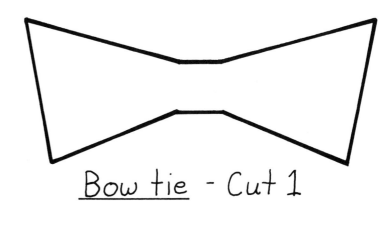

Bow tie - Cut 1

Fig. 1.9. Patterns for Gray Cloud.

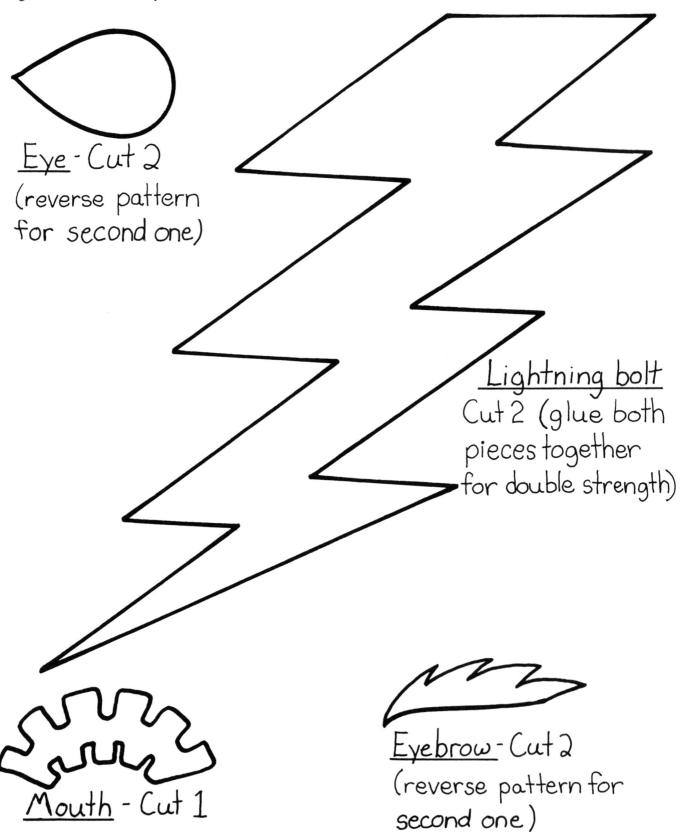

Eye - Cut 2
(reverse pattern
for second one)

Lightning bolt
Cut 2 (glue both
pieces together
for double strength)

Mouth - Cut 1

Eyebrow - Cut 2
(reverse pattern for
second one)

Fig. 1.10. Hold the rod near the bottom, out of sight of the audience.

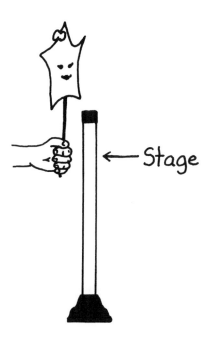

Fig. 1.11. Move a stick puppet up and down to indicate "yes" and rotate from side to side to indicate "no."

2

Felt Hand Puppets

ADVANTAGES OF FELT HAND PUPPETS

Felt hand puppets are easy to make. The use of felt has many advantages. It is durable and does not unravel; and new types of felt, such as Phun Phelt™, are thin, easy to sew, and do not stretch out of shape. As the puppeteer's thumb and fingers move the puppet's arms, this type of puppet is capable of displaying a wide range of emotions and actions. A felt hand puppet may pick up and carry props, wave, embrace another puppet, point, clap, rub its hands together, or shake a fist.

Perhaps the most important advantage of simple felt hand puppets is that one basic glove pattern may easily be transformed into male, female, child, adult, animal, or bird simply by the maker's choice of facial features, hair or fur, and clothing. Figure 2.1 shows some of the puppets used in "Star Light, Star Bright."

Fig. 2.1. Felt hand puppets used in "Star Light, Star Bright."

All the puppets shown for "The Town Mouse and the Country Mouse" (figure 2.2) are felt hand puppets. Patterns for making the puppets for these two shows are included in this chapter.

Fig. 2.2. Puppets used in "The Town Mouse and the Country Mouse."

CONSTRUCTION OF FELT HAND PUPPETS

The facial and clothing features may be sewn or glued onto the body of the puppet. A beige, brown, or peach-colored oval of felt may be used for the face, or facial features may be glued directly onto the body. These features may also be cut from iron-on tape, thus eliminating the need for gluing or sewing. Suggested trim includes ribbon, lace, eyelet, yarn, pipe cleaner, braid, sequins, rickrack, pompoms, and buttons. Thick looped yarn makes wonderful curly hair. Fake fur or yarn makes a nice lion's mane. The trim should reflect the character's personality. For example, Lucinda, the town mouse, is trimmed with lace, whereas Henry, the country mouse, wears only a simple felt bow tie. In a production of "The Town Mouse and the Country Mouse," it is not necessary to strive for realism in the color of the puppets. Instead, bright colors may be used to enhance the whimsy of the fairy tale. Thus, Henry may be green and Kitty bright red.

The following are general directions for the construction of a felt hand puppet. Specific patterns for the puppets used in "Star Light, Star Bright," "The Town Mouse and the Country Mouse," and "Percy's Tale" follow the instructions.

Materials Needed per Puppet

Two 9-by-11½-inch pieces of felt
Extra felt pieces for facial features, paws, and clothing
Other types of fabric for clothing (optional)
Trim (choose any appropriate for the puppet): lace, eyelet, braid, ribbon, yarn, pipe cleaner, sequins, rickrack, buttons, pompoms, cotton balls, or iron-on tape
Thread
Fabric craft glue
Sharp scissors
Sewing machine
Needle for hand sewing (optional)
Stapler (optional)
Iron (optional)

Method of Construction

The following is a step-by-step procedure for the construction of felt hand puppets. Reference to the illustrations will clarify the directions.

Cutting. Trace body pattern onto felt and cut two, using sharp scissors. Choose a pattern for ears, and trace and cut two. Ears may be lined with pink or beige felt by cutting two pieces slightly smaller than the ears (figure 2.3). Trace and cut oval for face, if desired.

Fig. 2.3. Placement of lining on ears.

Determine choice of facial features and pads for paws. Trace all patterns onto felt and cut out. Determine clothing needed, and trace and cut all pieces from felt or other fabric.

Face and trim. Place oval, if used, facial features, and clothing onto one body piece, layering eye pieces and mouth-nose combinations where necessary. Adjust placement, being sure eyes are not too high on the face and mouth is not too low (figure 2.4). Choose trim for clothing. Cut to proper size and place on the puppet (figure 2.5). Cut yarn to proper length for whiskers, if needed for animal puppet. (Or whiskers may be drawn onto the face with a thin marker after the other features are attached.)

Attach facial features, clothing, and trim to the puppet front piece. This may be done by gluing or hand sewing. If iron-on tape is used, follow the directions on the package. Allow any glue to dry thoroughly before further handling. Note: Hair is not attached at this time. Hair will be placed after the puppet body is sewn or glued together. After glue is dry, stitch yarn whiskers to the face with small hand stitches or with a sewing machine (figure 2.6). Experience has shown that glued-on yarn whiskers quickly fall off!

Tail. Determine material to be used for a tail, if desired. Three 9-inch pieces of yarn may be braided together to form a long tail for mice, lions, or cats. Pompoms or cotton balls serve well as rabbit tails. Pipe cleaner may be used for tails for mice or cats, and short curled pieces make good pig tails. Several feathers work well for the tail feathers of birds. Several straight pieces of yarn may be used together for horse or

Fig. 2.4. Placement of facial features, paw pads, and clothing. Ears will be added later.

Fig. 2.5. Placement of trim.

Fig. 2.6. Sew on yarn whiskers by machine or with small hand stitches.

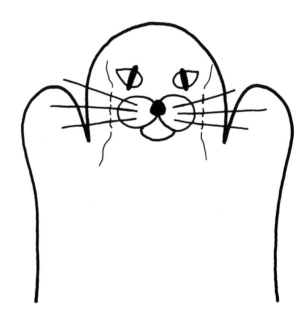

reindeer tails. Cotton, pompoms, and feathers may be glued onto the felt. Yarn tails, however, like yarn whiskers, should be sewn into place (figure 2.7). Pipe cleaner tails should be stapled or glued onto the felt.

Fig. 2.7. Tails may be fashioned from a variety of materials.

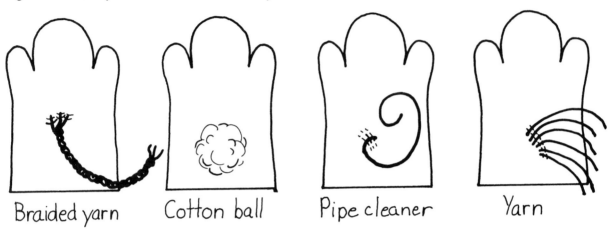

Braided yarn   Cotton ball   Pipe cleaner   Yarn

Attaching body pieces together. When glue is thoroughly dry, place the back body piece onto the work surface, tail side down. If body is to be glued together, place a thin bead of fabric craft glue around all edges except the bottom. Put ears into place with lower edges of ears slightly overlapping bead of glue. Place a bead of glue along lower edges of ears. Place front body piece on top of back, face up, aligning the two sections so edges match. Press together firmly and allow to dry thoroughly, preferably overnight. Pressure from a book or other heavy flat object will increase the staying power of the glue.

If body sections are to be sewn together, place front and back pieces together, right sides out. Slide the ear pieces into place between the two body pieces and pin into place. Pin body sections together. Stitch along all edges except bottom, sewing through all thicknesses. A zigzag or straight stitch may be used.

Head trim. Placement of hair, mane, or feathers is the final step. Choose straight or looped yarn for hair, fake fur or yarn for a mane, or feathers for a bird's head. Looped yarn trim, fake fur, and feathers may be glued or hand sewn to the top edge of the puppet. Straight yarn pieces, again, should be sewn into place as illustrated in figure 2.8.

Fig. 2.8. Stitching options for yarn hair. Yarn may be braided after being sewn.

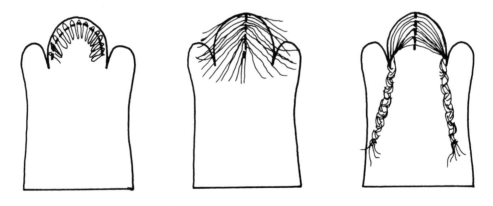

Other construction ideas. Felt puppets may be sprayed with Scotchguard™ to help prevent soiling or staining. Allow puppets to dry before handling.

Figures 2.9 through 2.15 provide pattern pieces to make the puppets for "The Town Mouse and the Country Mouse." Figures 2.16 through 2.18 provide patterns for the felt hand puppets used in "Star Light, Star Bright." Figures 2.19 through 2.24 provide patterns for puppets used in "Percy's Tale." The mouse for "Star Light, Star Bright" may be made from the pattern for Henry in "The Town Mouse and the Country Mouse." Figure 2.25 suggests other ideas for puppets.

Puppet makers may wish to create their own designs and patterns. It should be kept in mind that a puppet's face is incapable of changing expression. Thus, some thought should be put into the face one creates for a puppet. If a character is generally cheerful, a smile and slightly upturned eyes may add to that impression. If a character is generally scornful or mean, eyebrows that slant down toward the center or a pursed mouth will suggest this personality type.

MANIPULATION OF FELT HAND PUPPETS

The puppeteer operates a felt hand puppet by placing the fingers and thumb inside the head and arms of the puppet. One should experiment to find the method that is most comfortable. Figure 2.26 shows a variety of possible finger placements.

The puppeteer creates actions by moving the puppet's arms and head, by twisting the puppet from side to side, by bending at the wrist, or by moving the entire arm up and down or across the puppet stage. Details on puppet manipulation are supplied in part II, along with practice exercises for realistic movements.

(Text continues on page 39.)

Fig. 2.9. Pattern for felt hand puppet body (continued on page 23).

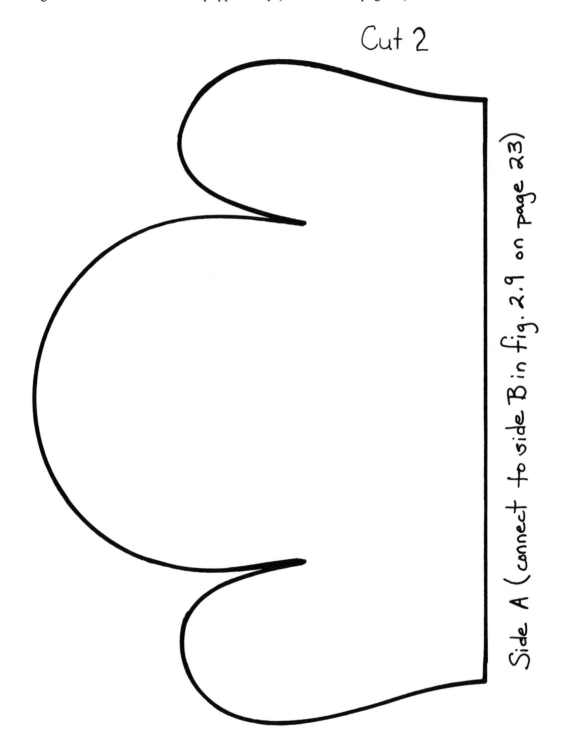

Cut 2

Side A (connect to side B in fig. 2.9 on page 23)

Side B (connect to side A on page 22)

Fig. 2.9. Pattern for felt hand puppet body.

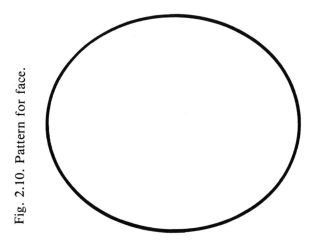

Fig. 2.10. Pattern for face.

Fig. 2.11. Patterns for Henry, the country mouse. Fashion a tail from three 9-inch pieces of yarn, braided together. Use six or eight 2-inch pieces of yarn or pipe cleaner for whiskers.

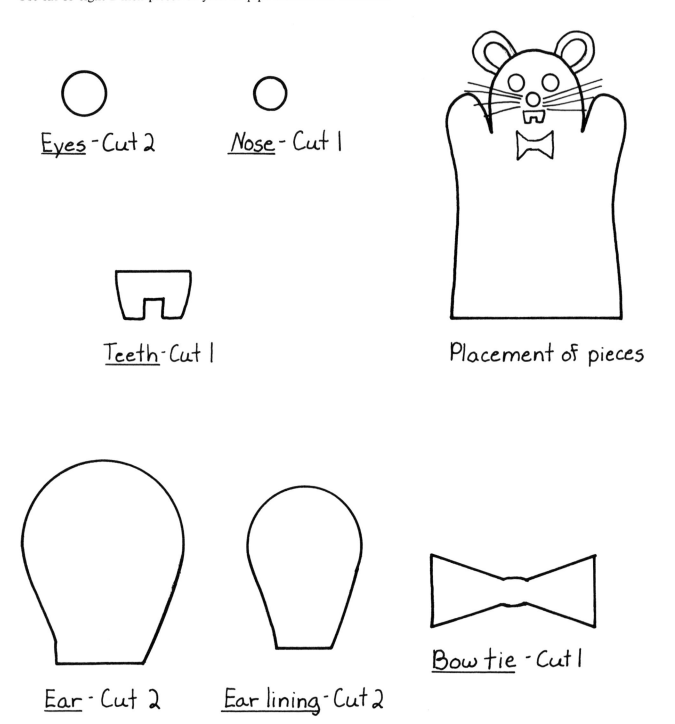

Eyes - Cut 2

Nose - Cut 1

Teeth - Cut 1

Placement of pieces

Ear - Cut 2

Ear lining - Cut 2

Bow tie - Cut 1

Fig. 2.12. Patterns for rabbit. Use a cotton ball for the tail. Make whiskers as for Henry.

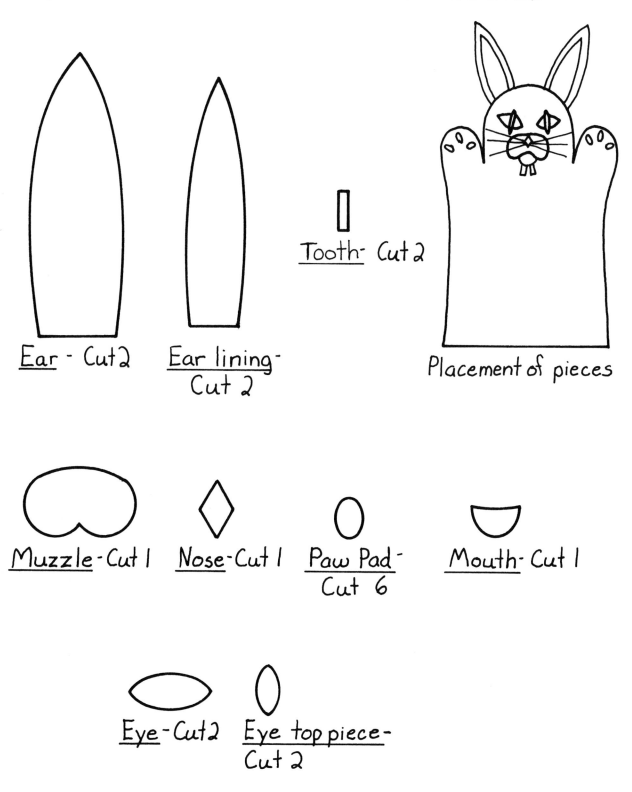

Ear - Cut 2   Ear lining - Cut 2   Tooth - Cut 2   Placement of pieces

Muzzle - Cut 1   Nose - Cut 1   Paw Pad - Cut 6   Mouth - Cut 1

Eye - Cut 2   Eye top piece - Cut 2

Fig. 2.13. Patterns for Lucinda, the town mouse. Use ear and eye patterns from fig. 2.11, Henry. Fashion a tail from a 6-inch piece of pipe cleaner. Make whiskers as for Henry. Use ½-inch- or 1-inch-wide eyelet or lace for apron straps, along top of apron and dress, and for skirt.

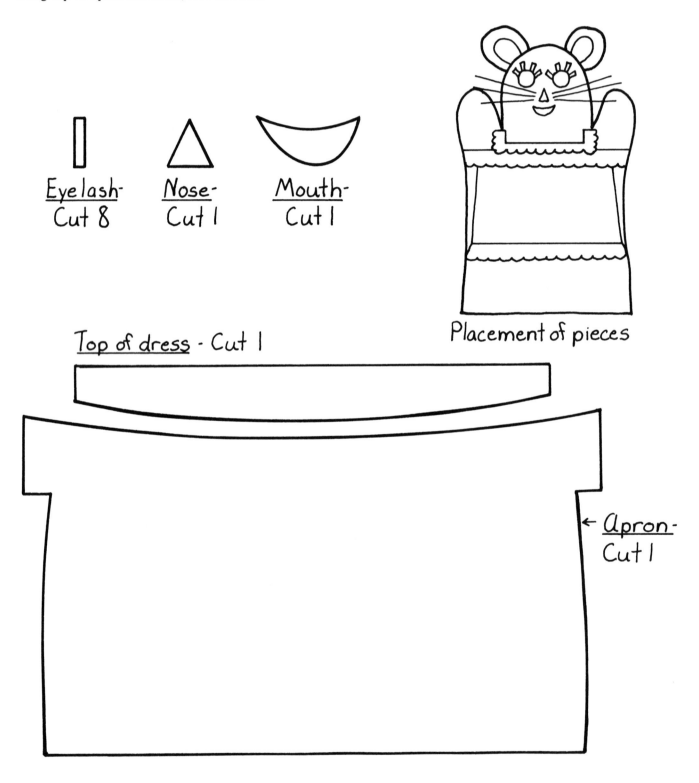

Eyelash- Cut 8

Nose- Cut 1

Mouth- Cut 1

Placement of pieces

Top of dress - Cut 1

← Apron- Cut 1

Fig. 2.14. Patterns for Mrs. Brown. Use eye and nose patterns from fig. 2.11, Henry. Use 1½-inch- or 2-inch-wide eyelet or lace for skirt. Make a bow from a 7-inch length of ribbon.

Mouth - Cut 1

Cheek - Cut 2

Placement of pieces

Blouse - Cut 1

Fig. 2.15. Patterns for Kitty. Use 1½-inch- or 2-inch-wide eyelet or lace for skirt. Make a tail from a 6-inch length of pipe cleaner, curled at the tip. Use six or eight 2-inch pieces of yarn for whiskers, or draw whiskers with thin black marker.

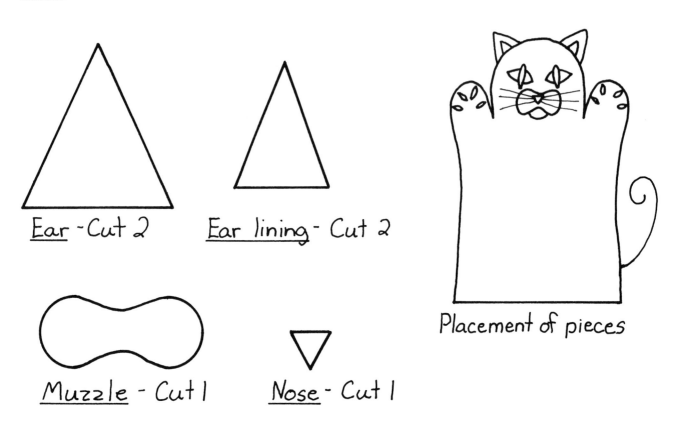

Ear - Cut 2

Ear lining - Cut 2

Placement of pieces

Muzzle - Cut 1

Nose - Cut 1

Eye - Cut 2

Eye top piece - Cut 2

Tongue - Cut 1

Claw - Cut 8

Fig. 2.16. Patterns for the lion. Use eye, nose, tongue, and muzzle patterns from fig. 2.15, Kitty. Fashion a braided tail from three 9-inch lengths of yarn. Use six or eight 2-inch pieces of yarn for whiskers.

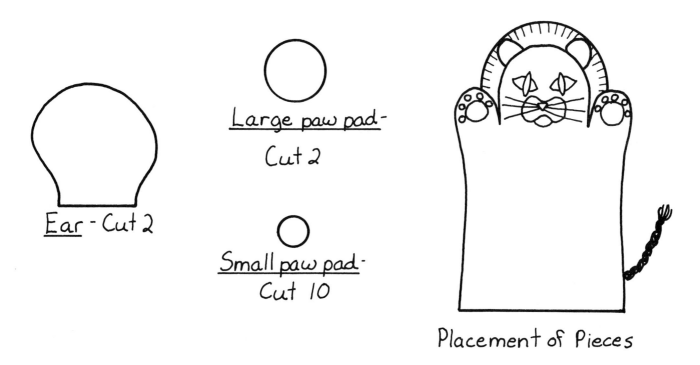

Ear - Cut 2

Large paw pad - Cut 2

Small paw pad - Cut 10

Placement of Pieces

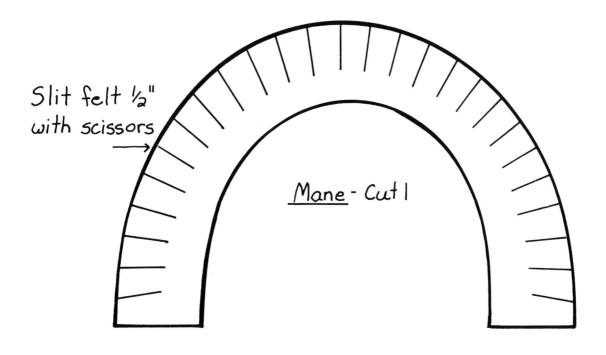

Slit felt ½" with scissors →

Mane - Cut 1

Fig. 2.17. Patterns for the reindeer. Make a tail from several 6-inch lengths of yarn. Back antlers with white cardboard for stiffness.

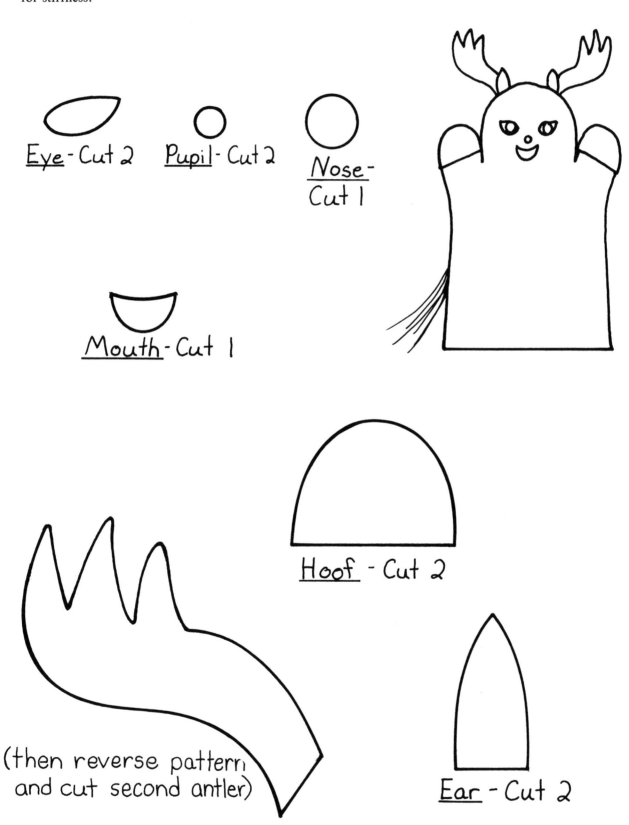

Eye - Cut 2   Pupil - Cut 2   Nose - Cut 1

Mouth - Cut 1

Hoof - Cut 2

(then reverse pattern and cut second antler)

Ear - Cut 2

Fig. 2.18. Patterns for Wendy. Use a 2-inch-wide piece of eyelet or lace for a skirt. Sew buttons onto blouse.

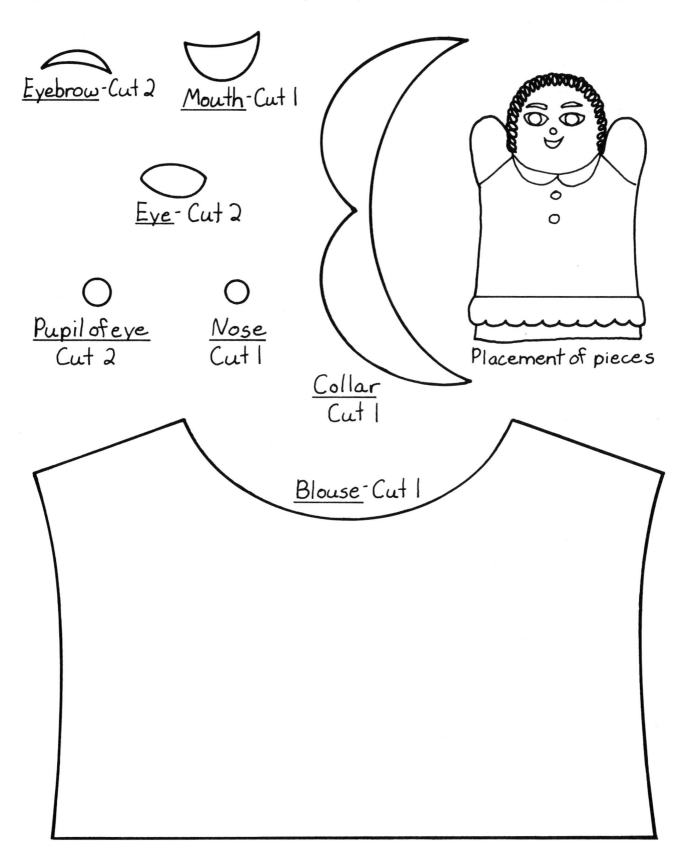

Eyebrow-Cut 2

Mouth-Cut 1

Eye-Cut 2

Pupil of eye
Cut 2

Nose
Cut 1

Collar
Cut 1

Placement of pieces

Blouse-Cut 1

Fig. 2.19. Patterns for Percy, the bookworm. Use eye and nose patterns from fig. 2.11, Henry, and mouth pattern from fig. 2.12, the rabbit. Cut segments from brightly colored fabric or felt and glue or sew onto puppet body.

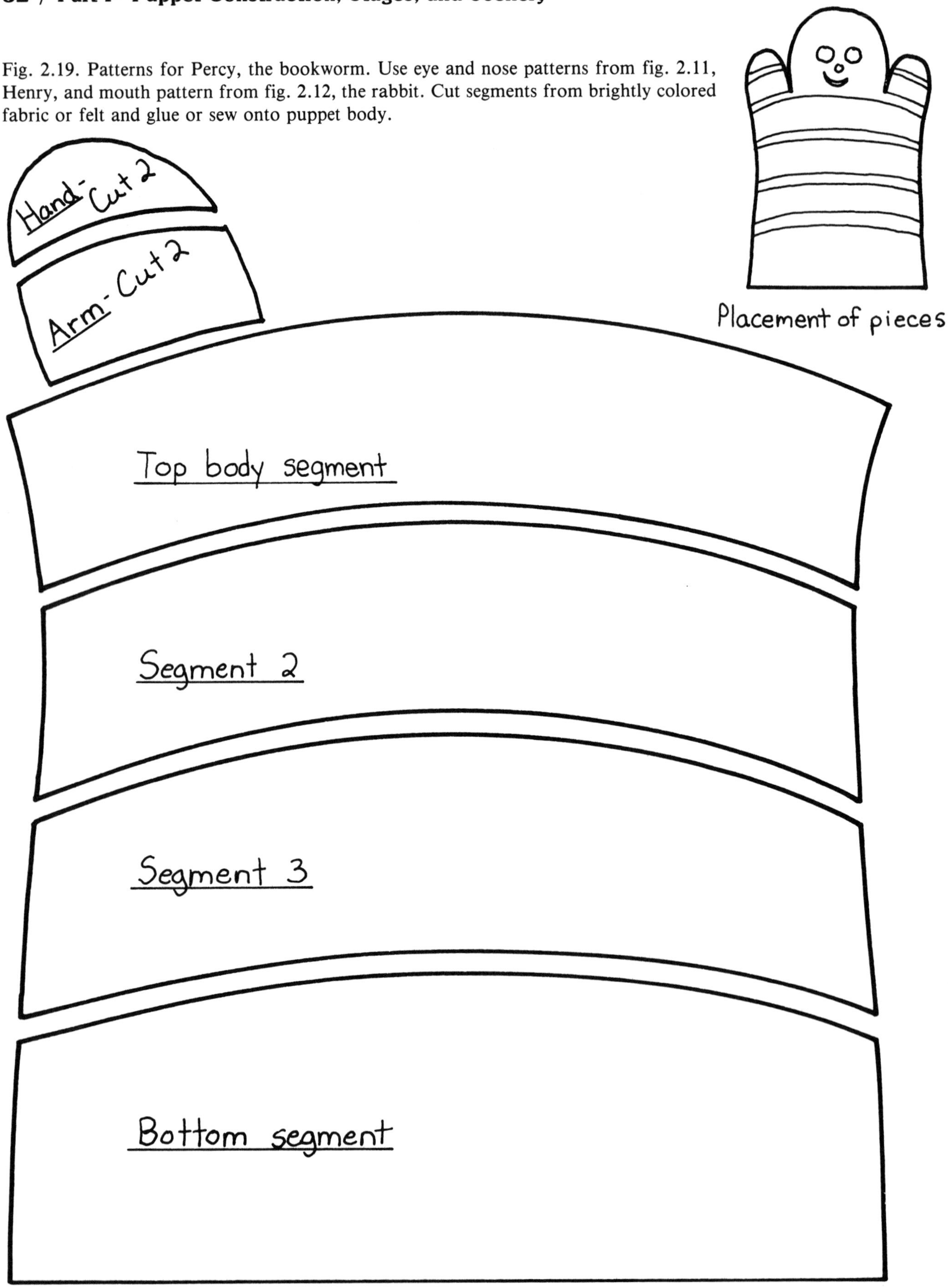

Hand-Cut 2

Arm-Cut 2

Placement of pieces

Top body segment

Segment 2

Segment 3

Bottom segment

Fig. 2.20. Pattern for Taran Tarantula. Use eye and nose patterns from fig. 2.11, Henry, and fig. 2.12, the rabbit. Use mouth pattern from figures 2.14, 2.17, or 2.18.

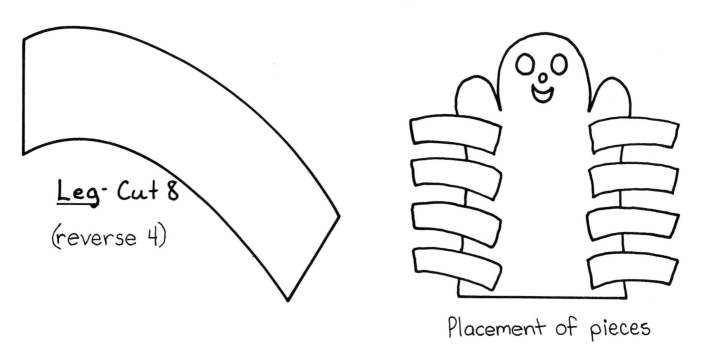

Leg - Cut 8

(reverse 4)

Placement of pieces

Fig. 2.21. Patterns for the bear. Use muzzle and tongue patterns from fig. 2.15, eye pattern from fig. 2.11, and paw pad patterns from fig. 2.16.

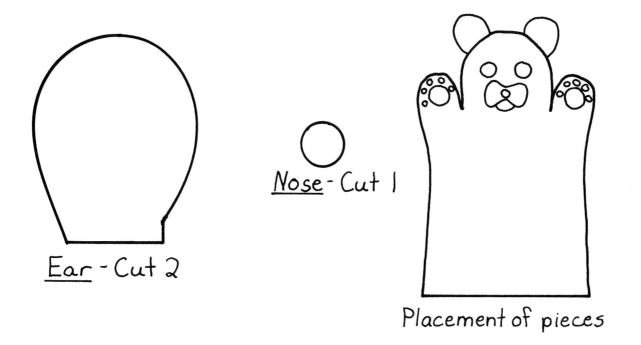

Ear - Cut 2

Nose - Cut 1

Placement of pieces

Fig. 2.22. Patterns for the wolf. Use paw pad patterns from fig. 2.16.

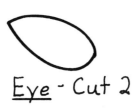

Eye - Cut 2

Pupil - Cut 2

Nose - Cut 1

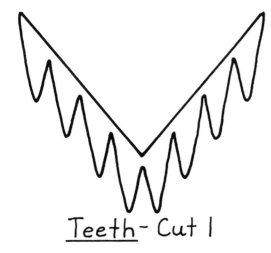

Teeth - Cut 1

Ear - Cut 2

Fig. 2.23. Patterns for the owl. Trim with feathers and, for eyelashes, bits of felt.

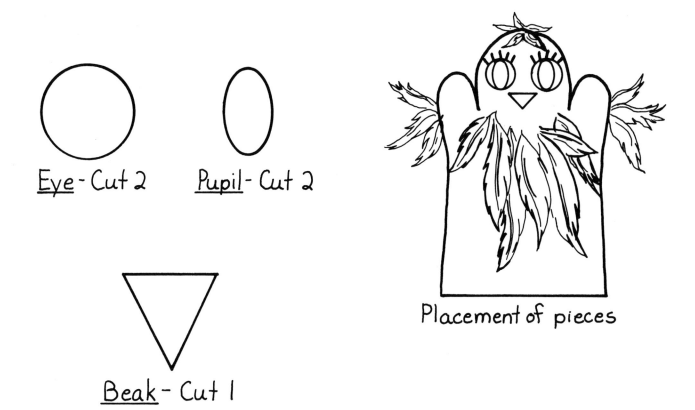

Eye - Cut 2   Pupil - Cut 2

Beak - Cut 1

Placement of pieces

Fig. 2.24. Patterns for the dragon. Use eye patterns from fig. 2.22, the wolf. Use claw patterns from fig. 2.15.

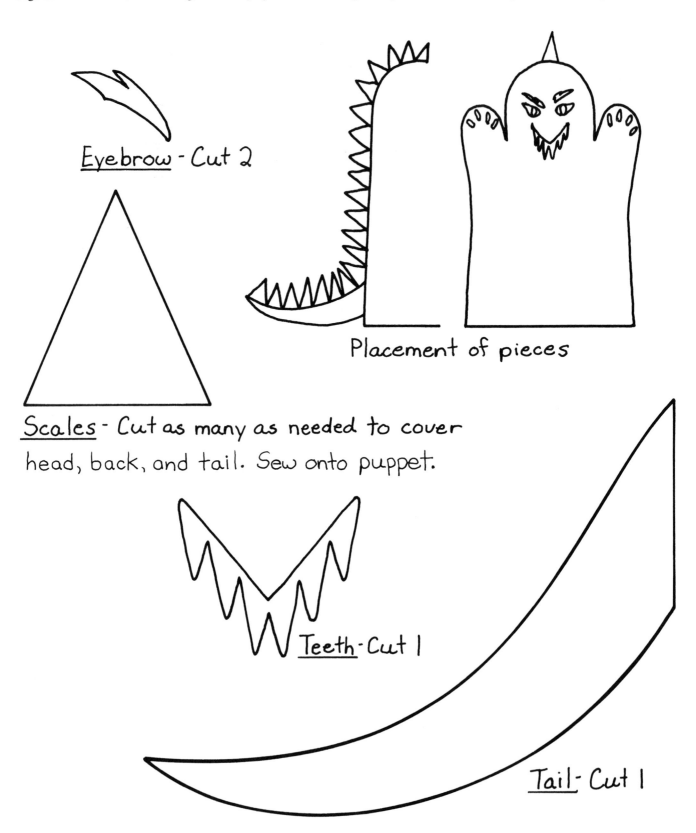

Eyebrow - Cut 2

Placement of pieces

Scales - Cut as many as needed to cover head, back, and tail. Sew onto puppet.

Teeth - Cut 1

Tail - Cut 1

Fig. 2.25. Ideas for additional felt hand puppets.

Princess   King   Pelican

Witch   Boy

Fig. 2.26. Hand placement options inside puppet.

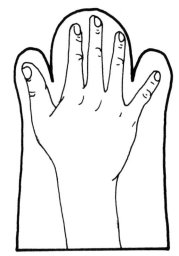

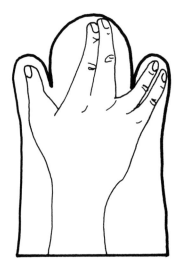

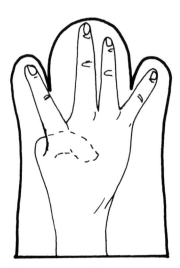

Thumb and little finger in arms; three fingers in head

Thumb in one arm; two fingers in head; two fingers in other arm

Pointer finger and little finger in arms; middle fingers in head; thumb folded over palm

3

Styrofoam Head Puppets

THE NATURE OF STYROFOAM HEAD PUPPETS

A third type of hand puppet is a cloth-bodied puppet with a head made from a sphere- or egg-shaped piece of Styrofoam. Stores that carry craft supplies may stock Styrofoam eggs and spheres in a variety of sizes. Like the felt puppets described in chapter 2, Styrofoam head puppets have arms operated by the puppeteer's fingers and thumb and thus may perform a broad range of gestures and actions. This type of puppet is more complicated to construct and involves sewing as well as gluing. Children will require help from an adult, and a workshop instructor may wish to have other adults handy to assist. Junior high and high school students, however, should be able to construct these puppets with a minimum of help, and the result will be a puppet of which the student will be truly proud.

CONSTRUCTION OF STYROFOAM HEAD PUPPETS

Styrofoam head puppet patterns are suggested for "The Forest Princess" (see part III, page 149). For simplicity, one body pattern is used for all the puppets. Individual character traits and differences are emphasized by the choice of fabric used for the costume. Thus, the queen's dress may be made of drapery brocade, the king's coat of red felt, and Felicia's and Pamela's dresses of plain cotton fabric. The bodies for the lion and the wolf may be made from a fabric called Care Bear Pile™, which is a soft orlon acrylic used in making stuffed animals. For the lion a light golden brown works well, and for the wolf a silvery gray. The bear cub may be made from a fake fur with a longer, reddish-brown pile. Fake fur is a nice material to use with children who are hand sewing, because the stitches, which become hidden in the pile, do not show. Another fabric that works well for animals is called doeskin. It is an imitation suede made of 100 percent polyester and also is known as doe suede or buck suede. It can be found in many fabric stores in tan, brown, and reddish-brown.

A puppet workshop provides a good opportunity for rummaging through leftover fabric scraps, buttons, and trims. Rickrack, lace, metallic trim, gold buttons, and plastic beads all can be used for the puppets in the cast of "The Forest Princess." Like the fabric, the trim should reflect the personality and traits of a character. Rottina, the self-centered princess, may wear a satin dress decorated with sequins, ribbon, and even Christmas tinsel. The king and prince wear medals made from metal buttons and ribbon scraps.

Sphere-shaped Styrofoam is used for the heads of the humans and the bear cub, and egg-shaped forms are used for the heads of the lion and the wolf. Turning the eggs onto their sides gives an elongated muzzle effect for the animals' faces.

Because Styrofoam tends to crumble as it is handled, it must be covered with an appropriate material. There are several techniques for creating the faces of puppets. One very effective way to represent skin is to cover the Styrofoam with two layers of gauze or cheesecloth and then paint the cloth with beige, brown, or peach-colored acrylic paint. The advantage of this technique is that facial features such as cheekbones, noses, and ears may be built onto the sphere, under the gauze, for a natural-looking face. Gauze and cheese-cloth stretch smoothly over the Styrofoam and are easy to manipulate.

An alternative technique is to cover the Styrofoam heads with papier-mâché and paint them when dry. As in the gauze technique, this technique allows the puppet maker to sculpt cheekbones, a nose, and ears. Libraries and craft stores carry books with instructions for working in papier-mâché.

For the animals, however, a softer more furry look is desired. It is difficult to use felt or fur to cover the Styrofoam eggs and spheres because these fabrics have limited stretch, and lumps and overlaps of the fabric result in very uneven, bumpy heads. Also, if the face is made of long-pile fur, the eyes, nose, and mouth can get lost in the fur—and to the audience the face may appear as a hairy mass instead of a character with a distinct look.

An easy method for beginners is to cover the Styrofoam with a man's thick sock. A sweatsock made of terrycloth gives a soft, furry look. If the sock has a terrycloth lining on the inside, simply turn it inside out before slipping it over the egg. The sock provides a good surface for sewing on buttons for eyes and noses and for gluing or sewing on felt and fur trim. The sock also provides some color variety. It is not necessary, or even desirable, to perfectly match the color of the sock to the color of the animal's body. A light yellow sock may be used for the face of the golden lion, a dark brown sock for the face of the reddish-brown bear, and a dark gray sock for the light gray wolf.

Hair for the people puppets may be fashioned from rug yarn, looped yarn, fake fur, or doeskin and may be glued directly to the fabric that covers the Styrofoam. One brand of looped yarn that works well is Maxi Loops™.

Instructions and patterns are provided for construction of the nine puppets used in "The Forest Princess." These instructions may be readily adapted to make the puppets needed for other shows—the wolf, prince, queen, and Felicia, for example, in "Little Red Riding Hood." Just give Felicia a red hooded cape and remove the crowns and medals from the prince and queen, and you'll have Red Riding Hood, the wolf, Grandma, and the woodcutter.

Materials Needed per Puppet

Two 14-by-16-inch pieces of fabric per puppet body

Suggestions:
    King: felt or brocade
    Queen: brocade, satin, velvet, or drapery fabric
    Prince: felt, velvet, or plain quilted fabric
    Felicia and Pamela: cotton, denim, calico, or broadcloth
    Rottina: satin, brocade, or velvet

    Animals: fake fur, doeskin, or felt
                NOTE: Extra fabric will be needed for trim to cover the animals' heads, to trim their faces, and to make tails. Animals will require at least ⅓ yard of 60-inch-wide fabric.

One 4-by-5-inch Styrofoam egg or one 4-inch sphere

One 6-by-10-inch piece of gauze or cheesecloth, plus a small number of extra pieces for building up facial features.

Acrylic paint for faces

Appropriate colors of felt or paint for eyes, eyebrows, nose, and mouth

Fake fur, doeskin, yarn, or yarn loops for hair

2½-by-3-inch pieces of felt for hands (in colors to complement or match faces)

Trim: ribbon for sashes and medals for king, queen, and prince; metal buttons for medals for king, queen, and prince; plastic or wooden buttons for eyes and noses and for costume trim; lace, eyelet, metallic trim, braid, rickrack, pompoms, plastic beads for costume trim

Two skeins heavy rug yarn for lion's mane

3-by-15-inch piece of cardboard for crown

Silver or gold foil paper to cover crown

Thread

Fabric craft glue

Five-minute epoxy glue

Scissors

Sharp knife

Sewing machine (optional)

Needle for hand sewing

Iron and ironing board

Method of Construction

The following instructions detail the procedures for the construction of Styrofoam head puppets.

Preparing the head. With a sharp knife, hollow out an opening in the Styrofoam sphere wide enough to insert two or three fingers and 2 to 3 inches deep (figure 3.1). Children should be supervised in this activity, or the instructor may wish to perform this step in advance. Care must be taken to make the opening deep enough so the puppet's head does not pop off the puppeteer's fingers when the puppet is manipulated. This causes the puppeteer to lose control of the puppet, and the puppet appears stooped and droopy. When using fake fur for the animals, cut the fingers holes slightly wider than needed because the furry necks will add thickness and will narrow the opening when the bodies are attached.

If using an egg-shaped piece of Styrofoam for a human oval-shaped face, the opening is made at the wider end. When using an egg shape for an animal's face, the opening is made on the side, toward the wider end. The narrow end becomes the animal's muzzle (figure 3.2).

Covering the styrofoam. One method is to cut off small pieces of *gauze or cheesecloth* and roll into balls for cheeks and nose; roll into ovals for ears, if desired. Fold the cloth lengthwise to form a doubled 6-by-5-inch piece. Stretch this over the sphere to cover the Styrofoam, tucking cheekbone, nose, and ear pieces into position beneath the cloth. Be sure the nose is centered on the face, with the cheekbones at approximately the same level as the nose, and the ears slightly higher. After adjusting the position of the facial features, carefully peel back the cheesecloth or gauze from the face, lift the facial features one at a time, and apply some glue to the back of each. Press back into place on the Styrofoam. Figure 3.3 helps clarify this step. Re-cover the sphere with the cloth, apply glue to the inside of the finger opening, and tuck excess cloth up inside the opening, pressing firmly. With gentle strokes, paint the entire sphere an appropriate flesh color.

Fig. 3.1. Hollow out an opening in the Styrofoam sphere.

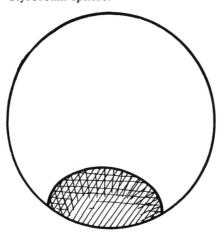

Fig. 3.2. To create an animal head, place the opening on the side, toward the wider end.

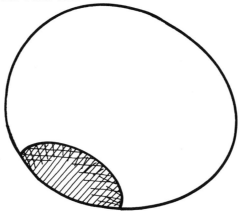

Fig. 3.3. Gauze is peeled back, and cheekbones, nose, and ears are glued into place. Then gauze is stretched back over the sphere, tucked up into the finger hole and glued inside the opening.

A second method is to use a *sock covering*. But before covering the Styrofoam egg for the head of a wolf or any animal needing a long muzzle, use a sharp knife to carve a pointed muzzle on the narrow end, as indicated in figure 3.4. The nose may be further lengthened by gluing a rolled-up piece of polyester filling (or extra portion of leftover sock) onto the end of the muzzle. Cut off the top of a heavy terrycloth sock approximately 1 inch below the ribbing. Slip the sock over the egg with the heel section stretched over the top of the animal's head (figure 3.5). Build up the animal's head by folding the leftover sock ribbing lengthwise and tucking it under the sock in the heel area above and behind the muzzle. Extra polyester filling may be added to build a higher head (figure 3.6). With scissors, slit the sock along the bottom of the egg to reveal the finger hole (figure 3.7). Cover the inside of the finger opening with craft glue, and tuck in the ends of the sock, overlapping at the back of the head where necessary (figure 3.8).

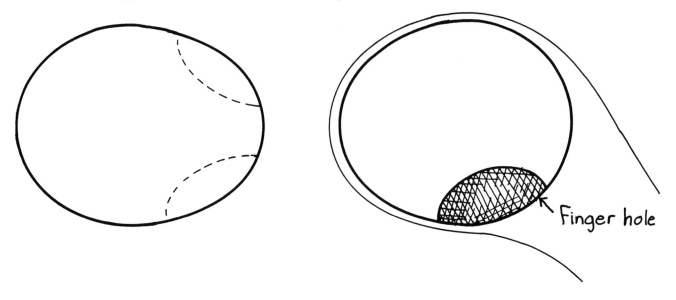

Fig. 3.4. Carve a pointed animal muzzle at the narrow end of the egg.

Fig. 3.5. Stretch the sock over the egg with the heel at the top of the head.

Fig. 3.6. Leftover portion of sock plus polyester batting are used to build up the animal's head.

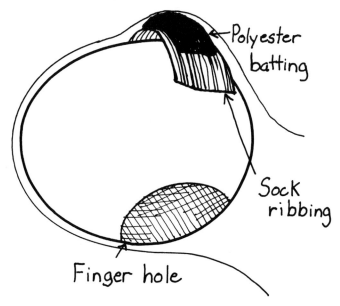

Facial trim. If fabric has been painted a flesh color, allow it to dry thoroughly before continuing. Eyes, eyebrows, and mouth may then be painted directly onto the face. Light pencil drawings may be made on the face before painting to determine the placement of features. Or facial features may be fashioned from felt and buttons. Trace the pattern pieces onto felt and cut out. Eyebrows and mustaches may be cut from doe-skin or fake fur. Large buttons may serve as eyes, or small buttons may be sewn over felt pieces, as in figure 3.9. Determine placement of facial features, and glue or sew into place. See the patterns provided at the end of this chapter for specific animal and people faces. Step-by-step directions are given for the animal faces immediately following the patterns, as each animal is constructed in a slightly different manner.

Fig. 3.7. Slit the sock to reveal the finger opening.

Fig. 3.8. Glue the ends of the sock up inside the opening, overlapping at the back of the head.

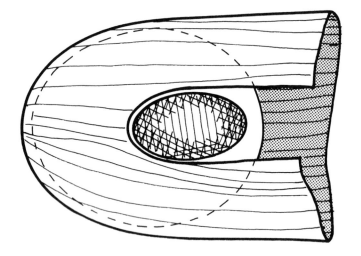

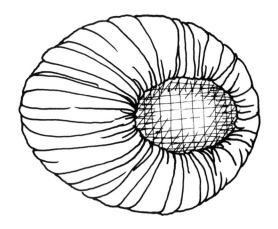

Fig. 3.9. Eyes may be created with buttons sewn or glued over felt pieces.

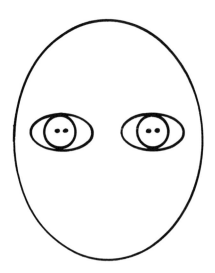

Hair. Hair for human characters may be fashioned from yarn, Maxi Loops, or fake fur and glued into place (see figures 3.10-3.15). A yarn wig may be made in the following manner. Cut a piece of cardboard 8 inches wide and as long as the wig is to be on each side. Wind yarn lengthwise around the cardboard the entire width. Down the center of one side stitch the yarn together, looping the thread tightly around two or three strands of yarn at a time (figure 3.15). On the opposite side of the cardboard, cut the yarn through the center. The wig may be trimmed to even the ends. A long wig may be braided. The wig should be glued securely into place on the head.

(Text continues on page 47.)

Fig. 3.10. For the queen, thick craft yarn is wound around the head, starting at the center back.

Fig. 3.11. For the king, three rows of acrylic loops are glued around the back of the head.

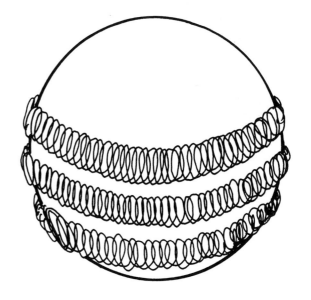

Fig. 3.12. For Felicia, acrylic loops are glued vertically from the forehead, over the back of the head to the neck.

Fig. 3.13. The prince's hair, eyebrows, and mustache may be made from short-napped fake fur glued to the head.

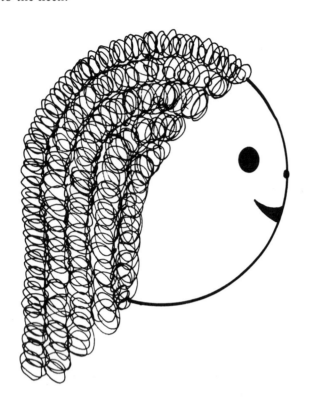

Fig. 3.14. Pamela may wear a braided wig.

Fig. 3.15. To make a braided wig, wind yarn lengthwise around an 8-inch piece of cardboard. Stitch the yarn together down the center of one side. Cut the yarn off the cardboard on the other side, directly opposite the stitches.

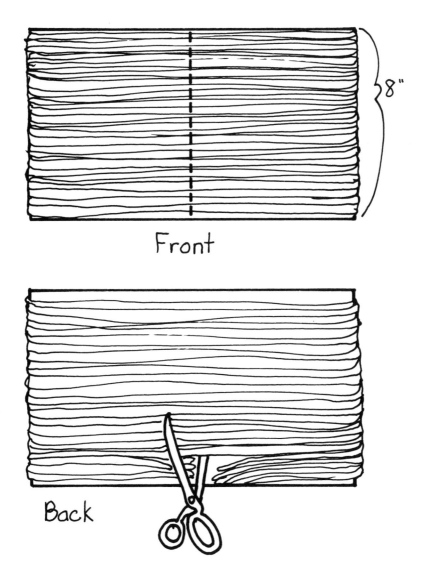

Front

Back

Puppet body. While the glue on the head is drying, the body of the puppet may be made. Trace the body pattern onto the fabric, and cut out two pieces. For animal bodies, cut along rounded ends for paws as indicated on the pattern. If fabric with a pile or nap is used, attention must be paid to the direction in which the fur lies. Animal fur should run from the top (neck) to the bottom of the puppet. The pattern, then, must be placed on the fabric in the proper direction. If not careful, one may end up with a wolf whose gorgeous silver fur runs sideways in the front and upside down in the back!

For people puppets, trace hand pattern onto felt and cut four pieces. Match two hand sections and sew together very close to the edges by hand or machine, using matching thread. The added thickness and weight of a doubled hand piece will help prevent the hand from flopping back and forth.

With the right sides of the fabric together, join the two body sections by stitching about ½ inch from the edges, being sure to leave the entire bottom and top of the neck unstitched. If hands are to be included for people, before stitching, pin them into place at the wrist between the two body pieces, with the fingers pointing in toward the body of the puppet (figure 3.16). Pin body sections together and join, stitching over the edge of each hand, as shown in figure 3.16. Be careful not to catch the puppet fingers or thumb in the stitching. This is probably the most difficult part of the construction process. For this reason, an instructor working with children may want to construct the bodies before the workshop begins. Sewing tiny fingers may prove tedious, and one may wish to give up and glue the body together. If this feeling begins to grow, don't give in. The puppet will be much more durable if it is sewn together.

Hem the bottom of the puppet by folding up ½ inch toward the wrong side of the fabric. Stitch by hand or machine. Felt puppets do not require hemming. With scissors, clip the curves at the sides of the body, being careful not to cut through the stitching (figure 3.17). Turn the puppet right side out and press with an iron.

Tails for the animals may be made from felt, yarn, or large pompoms and sewn by hand or glued into place. See figures 3.18-3.25 for instructions and suggestions.

(Text continues on page 53.)

Fig. 3.16. Place body sections right sides together with hand pieces between them, fingers pointing in. Stitch around sides, arms, and sides of neck.

Fig. 3.17. Clip curves before turning body right side out.

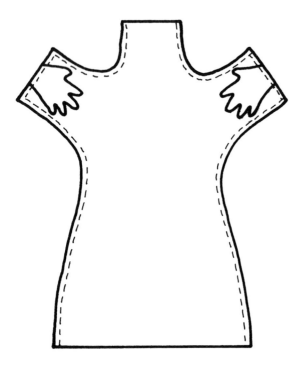

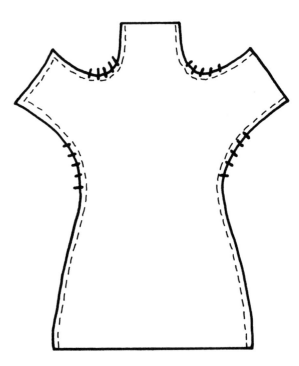

Fig. 3.18. For the lion, cut a tail from fake fur, using pattern. Fold in half lengthwise and stitch along long edge and one end. Or cut a piece of felt 8 inches long and 1 inch wide.

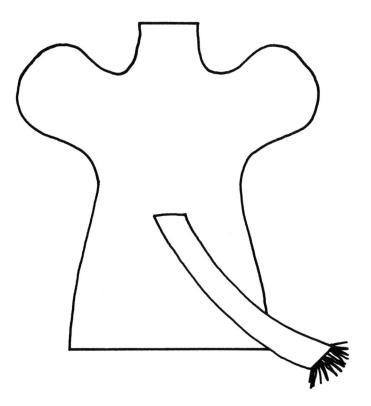

Fig. 3.19. Cut ten to twelve 6-inch lengths of yarn. Fold yarn in half and sew to one end of the tail along folds.

Fig. 3.20. Sew tail to the lion's body on underside of tail to give it some lift. Flip tail down into position.

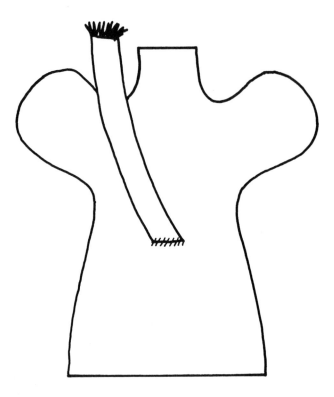

Fig. 3.21. For the wolf, cut a tail from fake fur, using pattern.

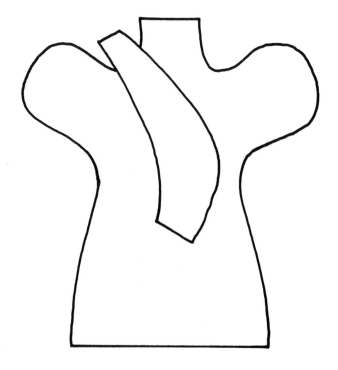

Fig. 3.22. Bend a piece of wire or coat hanger as shown.

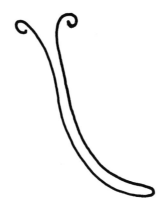

Fig. 3.23. Poke ends of wire through a hole in the body where base of tail will be. Sew wire to the body as shown. The stitches will not be noticeable in the fur.

(Inside back body piece)

Fig. 3.24. Fold tail in half lengthwise and sew together along long edge and tip, leaving base of tail open. Slip tail over wire and attach with hand stitches onto body.

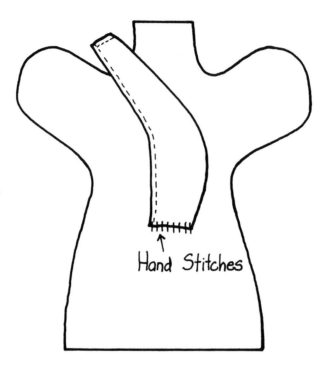

Fig. 3.25. Bend the wire so that the tail curves upward.

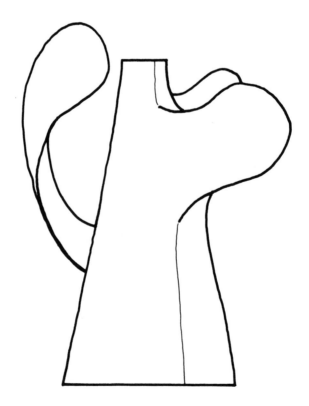

Costume decoration. Decorate the puppet's costume by gluing or hand sewing trim such as ribbon, buttons, lace, braid, sequins, or rickrack. For ideas refer to the illustrations of the puppets from "The Forest Princess" later in this chapter. As previously discussed, costume trim should be in keeping with the traits and personality of the individual character. Rottina may be made flamboyant with metallic trim, tinsel, or even feathers. Felicia may wear a simple eyelet yoke and plastic buttons. The members of the royal family wear medals and crowns. A pattern is provided for the crowns, which may be cut from cardboard and covered with foil paper. The crowns may be secured to the heads with straight pins or with pearl-trimmed head pins available in fabric and craft stores. Sequins, beads, and buttons may be glued to the crowns for a jeweled effect. Animal paws may be decorated with felt pads or claws glued to the front of each paw. Patterns for these are provided later in this chapter.

Although suggestions are included for the design of the "Forest Princess" puppets, keep in mind that decorating the costumes and faces is one of the most interesting and enjoyable aspects of puppet making and that puppet makers may wish to develop their own designs. Individual creativity should be encouraged in a puppet workshop. There may be as many ways of making a prince puppet as there are puppet makers.

Puppet makers should remember that the puppets must be seen from a distance by the audience. Thus, large designs and color contrasts work best. Minute beading and fancy stitches will be seen only by the puppeteers and will not add to the enjoyment of the audience members.

Final assembly. When the glue and paint on costumes and heads are dry, the puppets may be assembled. Glue the neck of the costume up inside the finger hole in the head, pressing the fabric firmly to the Styrofoam. Fabric craft glue will hold well.

MANIPULATION OF PUPPETS

Cloth-bodied, Styrofoam-head puppets are manipulated in much the same manner as are the felt puppets in chapter 2. Two or three fingers are placed inside the puppet's head. The puppeteer moves the puppet's head, arms, or entire body to represent the emotions that accompany the words. Posture adds to the actions and words. These puppets may bend their necks, stoop, straighten up, twist, or look up. Practice with the puppets will result in realistic gestures and movements. Carefully made, and manipulated with clear and deliberate motions, these puppets will add to the delight of the audience as well as to the enjoyment of the puppeteers.

Patterns, Suggestions, and Further Directions
for Specific Puppets

The following patterns are for use with 4-inch Styrofoam spheres (for the people puppets and the bear cub) and 4-by-5-inch eggs (for the wolf and the lion). Patterns will have to be adjusted if smaller or larger heads are desired. Figures 3.26-3.54 provide the patterns, photographs, and directions.

(Text continues on page 78.)

Fig. 3.26. Body pattern for Styrofoam head puppet (continued on page 55).

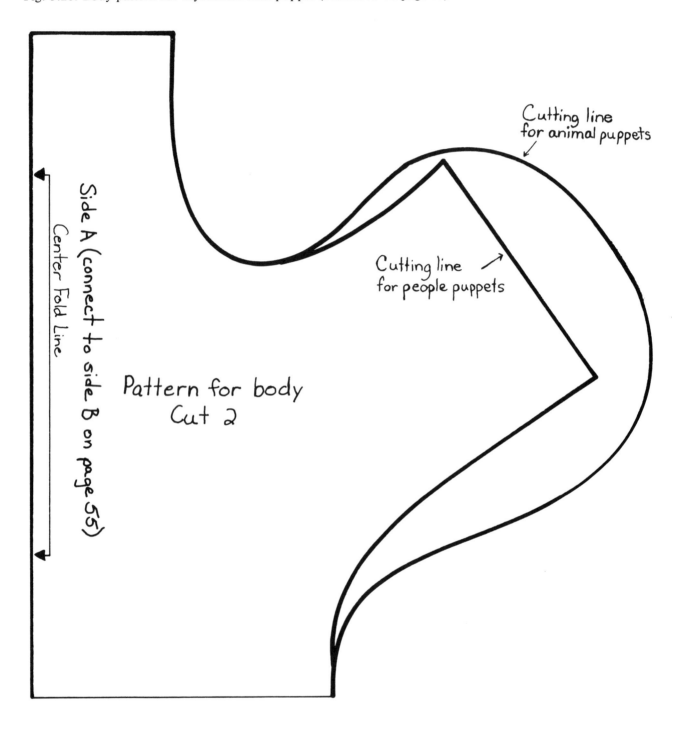

Side A (connect to side B on page 55)

Center Fold Line

Pattern for body
Cut 2

Cutting line
for animal puppets

Cutting line
for people puppets

Fig. 3.26. Body pattern for Styrofoam head puppet.

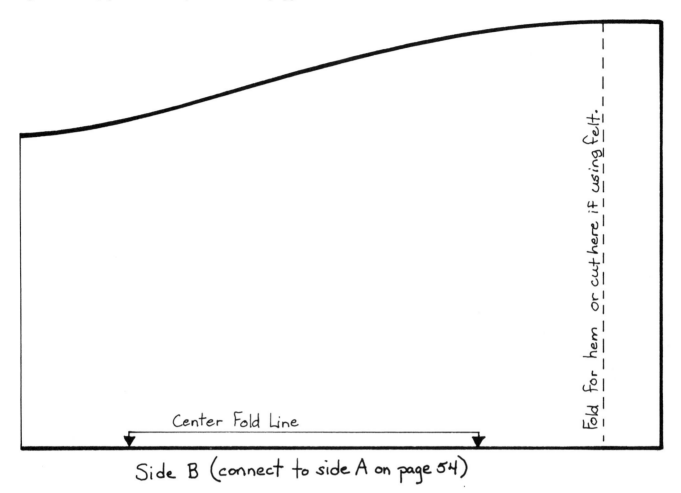

Center Fold Line

Fold for hem or cut here if using felt.

Side B (connect to side A on page 54)

Fig. 3.27. Pattern for hand.

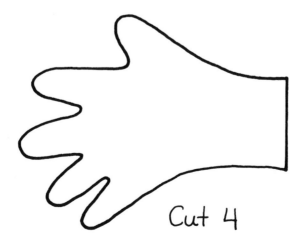

Cut 4

Fig. 3.28. Pattern for crown.

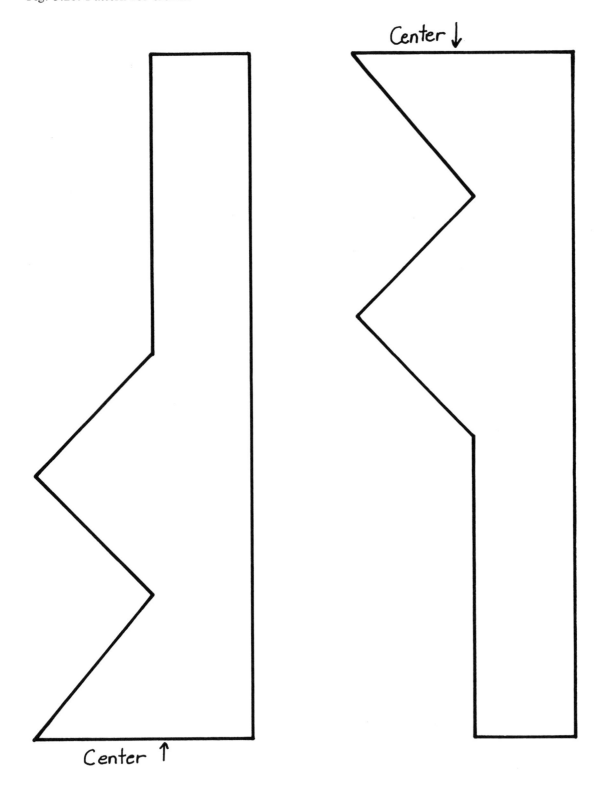

Fig. 3.29. The king, from "The Forest Princess."

Fig. 3.30. Patterns and suggestions for the king. Materials needed: two flat ½-inch buttons, felt scraps, one 2-inch piece of looped yarn, and epoxy. Mustache is made from a 2-inch piece of looped yarn. Nose may be molded under gauze covering or cut from felt and glued to the face. For eye, glue on button with epoxy, overlapping eyelid.

Eyelid - Cut 2

Nose - Cut 1

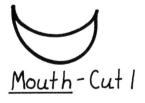

Mouth - Cut 1

Placement of eye pieces

Fig. 3.31. The queen, from "The Forest Princess."

Fig. 3.32. Pattens and suggestions for the queen. Materials needed: two ½-inch black buttons, felt scraps, and epoxy. Eye is made as for the king.

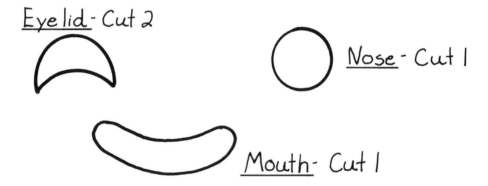

Fig. 3.33. The prince, from "The Forest Princess."

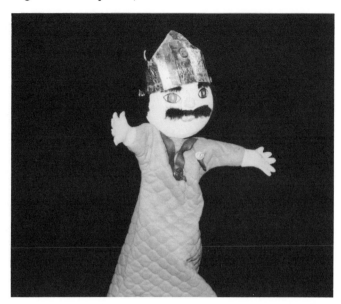

Fig. 3.34. Patterns and suggestions for the prince. Materials needed: felt scraps and brown doeskin or felt.

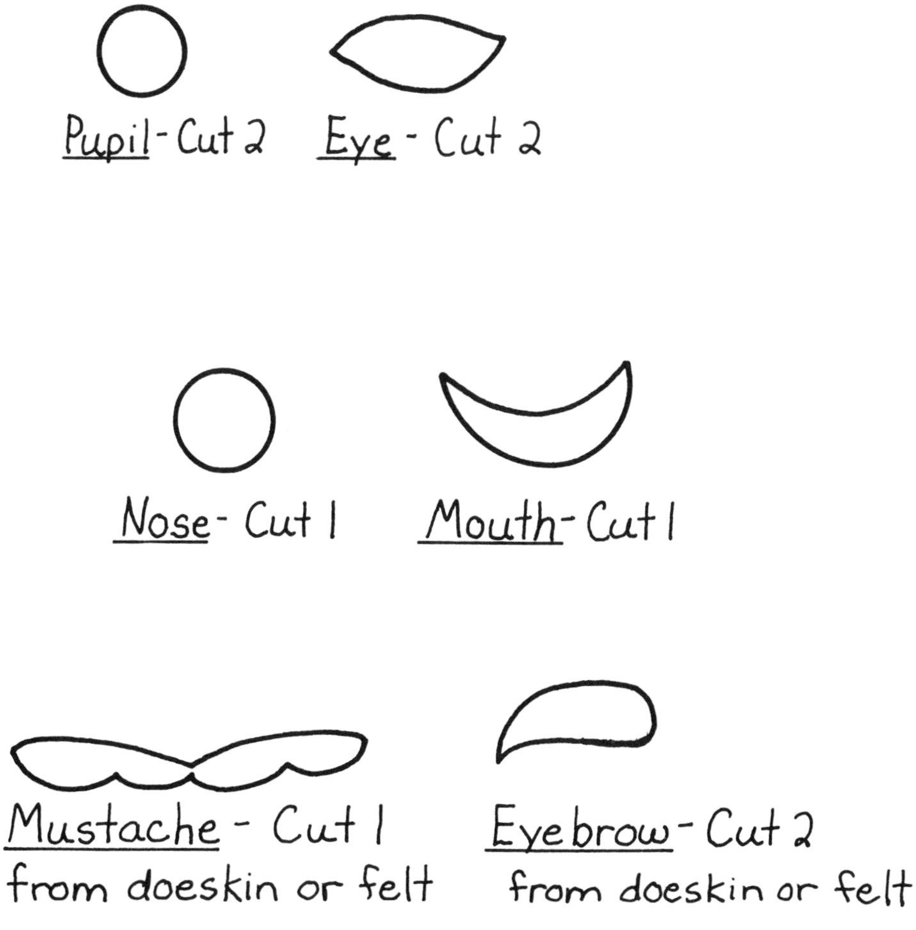

<u>Pupil</u>- Cut 2   <u>Eye</u> - Cut 2

<u>Nose</u>- Cut 1   <u>Mouth</u>- Cut 1

<u>Mustache</u> - Cut 1
from doeskin or felt

<u>Eyebrow</u>- Cut 2
from doeskin or felt

Fig. 3.35. Felicia, from "The Forest Princess."

Fig. 3.36. Patterns and suggestions for Felicia. Materials needed: two ½-inch violet, blue, or green buttons; felt scraps; and epoxy.

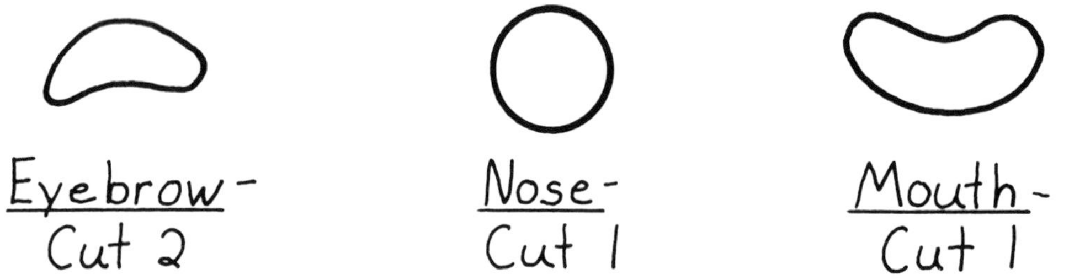

Eyebrow-
Cut 2

Nose-
Cut 1

Mouth-
Cut 1

Fig. 3.37. Pamela, from "The Forest Princess."

Fig. 3.38. Patterns and suggestions for Pamela. Materials needed: two ⅜-inch buttons, felt scraps, and epoxy. For mouth, use pattern for the prince.

Eyebrow-
Cut 2

Nose-
Cut 1

Fig. 3.39. Rottina, from "The Forest Princess."

Fig. 3.40. Patterns and suggestions for Rottina. Materials needed: felt scraps. For eyes, use patterns for the prince.

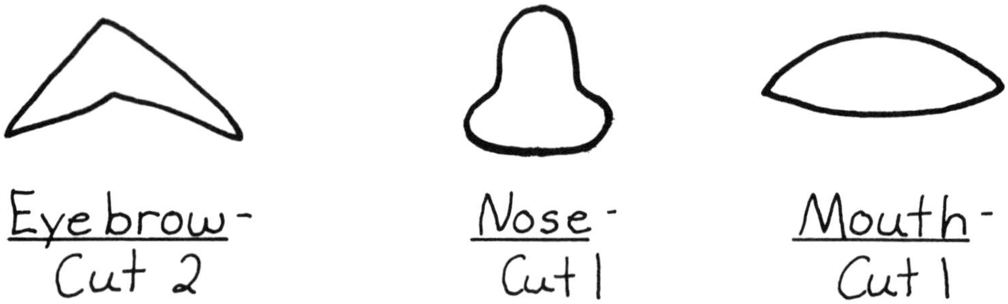

Eyebrow-
Cut 2

Nose-
Cut 1

Mouth-
Cut 1

Fig. 3.41. Wolf, from "The Forest Princess" (continued on pages 64-66).

Fig. 3.42. Patterns and suggestions for the wolf. Materials needed: fake fur to match body, one 1½-inch black button for nose, and felt scraps (black, brown, yellow, white, red). (Fig. 3.42 continues to page 66.)

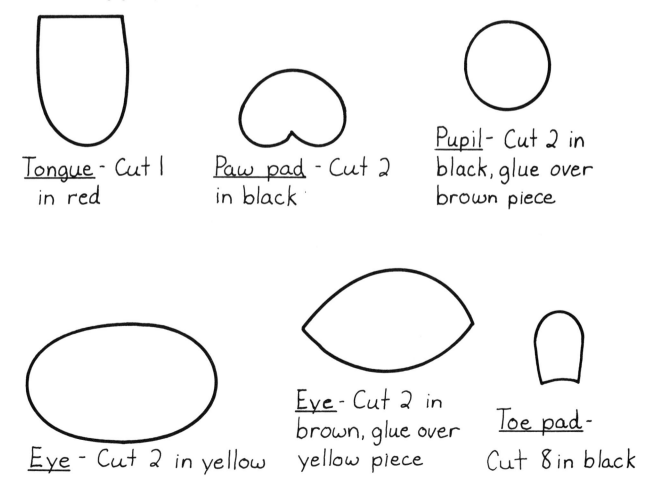

Tongue - Cut 1 in red

Paw pad - Cut 2 in black

Pupil - Cut 2 in black, glue over brown piece

Eye - Cut 2 in yellow

Eye - Cut 2 in brown, glue over yellow piece

Toe pad - Cut 8 in black

Fig. 3.42. Patterns and suggestions for the wolf.

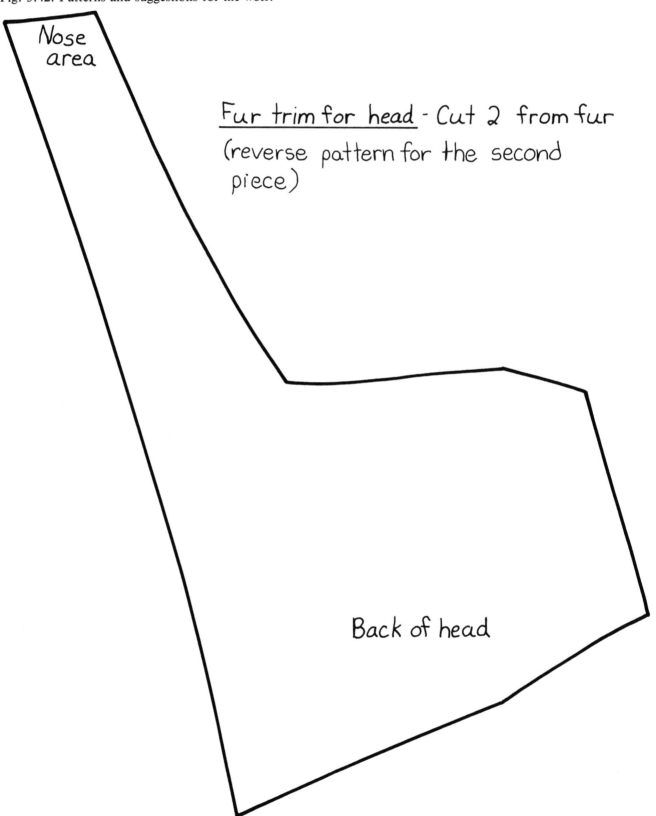

Fig. 3.42. Patterns and suggestions for the wolf.

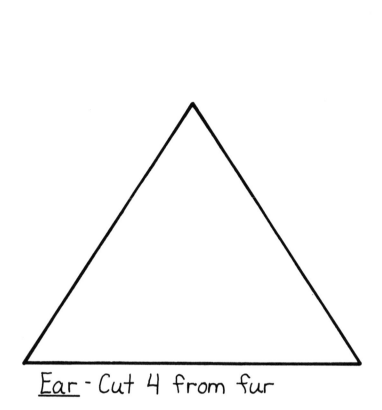

Eyebrow - Cut 2 from fur (reverse the pattern for second piece)

Ear - Cut 4 from fur

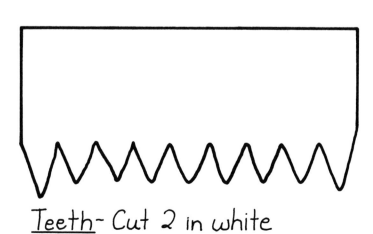

Teeth- Cut 2 in white

Fig. 3.42. Patterns and suggestions for the wolf.

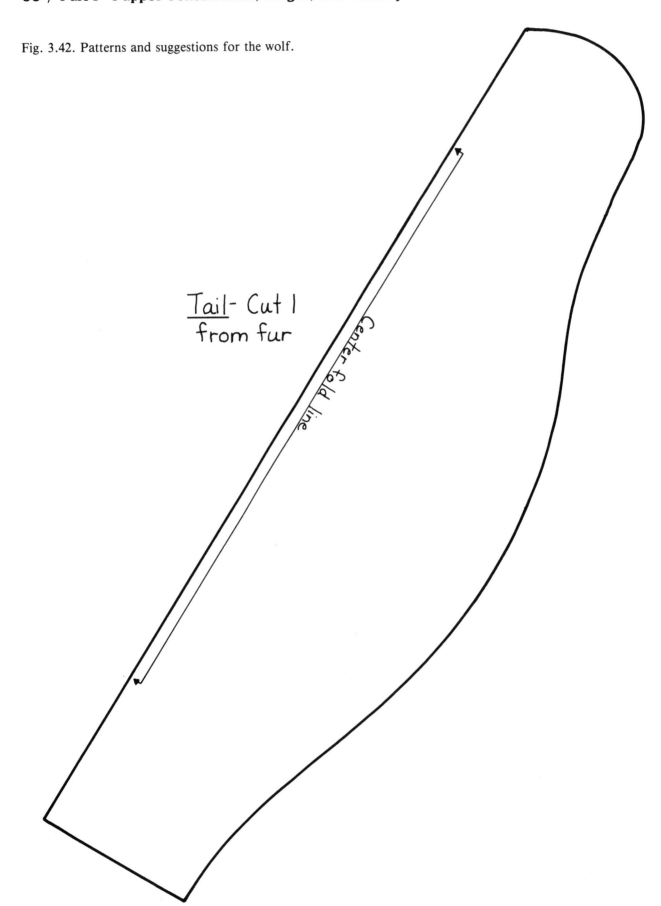

Tail- Cut 1
from fur

Center fold line

Fig. 3.43. Sew on fur trim along wolf's jaw.

Fig. 3.44. Bear Cub.

Fig. 3.45. Patterns and suggestions for the bear cub. Materials needed: fake fur to match body, one 1½-inch pompom for muzzle (slightly lighter in color than the face), three 9/16-inch dark brown buttons for eyes and nose, and felt scraps in a color similar to that of muzzle, or black. (Fig. 3.45 continues to page 71.)

Covering for top of head -
Cut 1 from fur

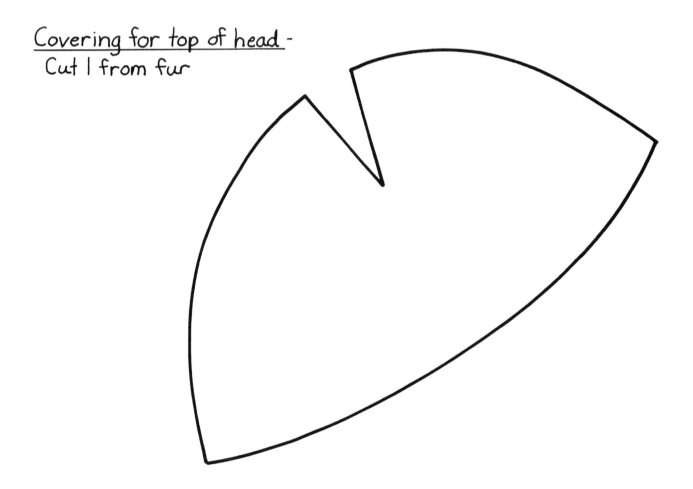

Fig. 3.45. Patterns and suggestions for the bear cub.

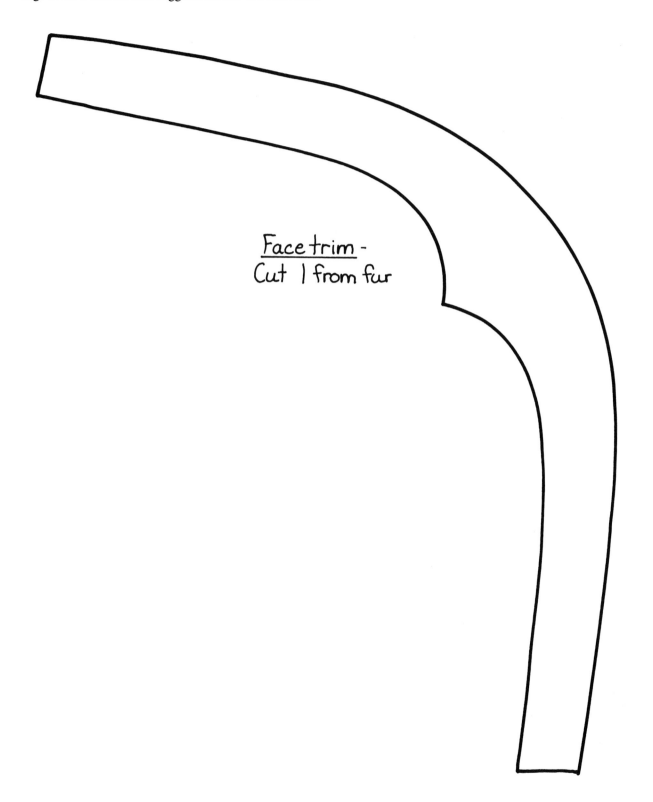

Face trim -
Cut 1 from fur

Fig. 3.45. Patterns and suggestions for the bear cub.

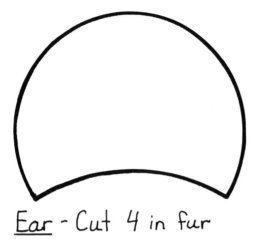

Ear - Cut 4 in fur

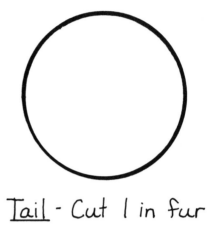

Tail - Cut 1 in fur

Paw pad - Cut 2 in color similar to muzzle or in black

Claw - Cut 10 to match paw pads

Fig. 3.45. Patterns and suggestions for the bear cub.

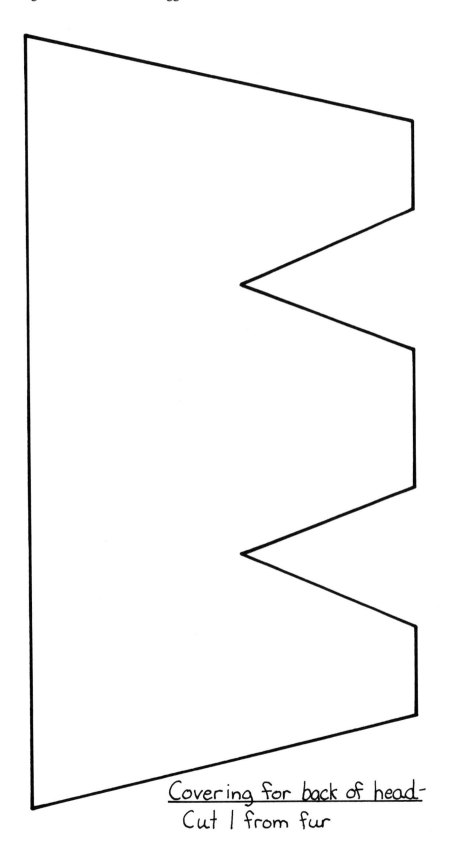

Covering for back of head-
Cut 1 from fur

Fig. 3.46. Sew on covering for back of head, bringing V-shaped cutout edges together at neck area.

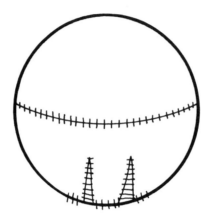

Fig. 3.47. Sew on covering for top of head, slightly overlapping piece for back of head, bringing V-shaped cutout edges together.

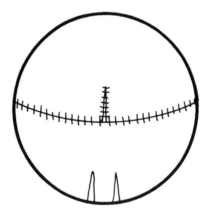

Fig. 3.48. Sew on face trim, matching edges with trim from the back and top of head.

Fig. 3.49. Leo, the Lion.

Fig. 3.50. Patterns and suggestions for the lion. Materials needed: fake fur to match body, felt scraps (black, green, gold, red, brown), one 1½-inch button for nose if desired, two skeins heavy rug yarn (suggested colors: one gold and one natural) (continued on page 75).

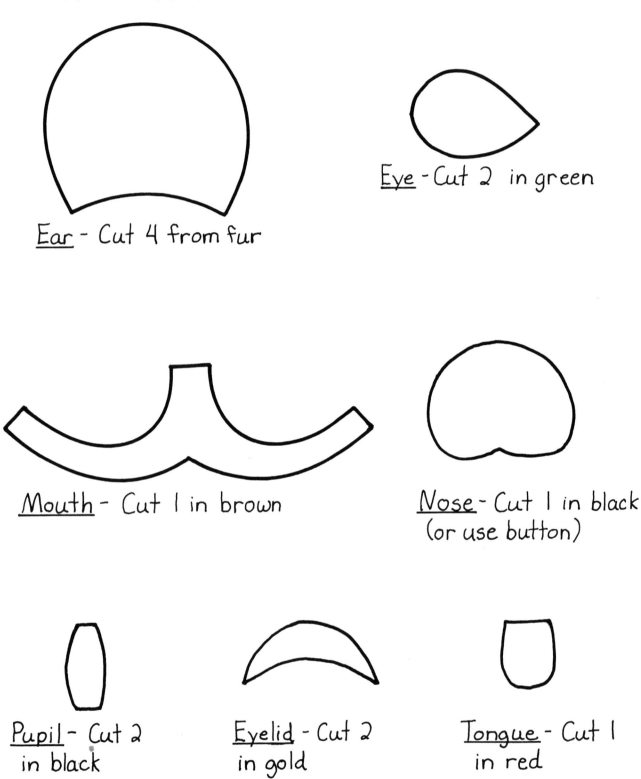

Ear - Cut 4 from fur

Eye - Cut 2 in green

Mouth - Cut 1 in brown

Nose - Cut 1 in black
(or use button)

Pupil - Cut 2
in black

Eyelid - Cut 2
in gold

Tongue - Cut 1
in red

Fig. 3.50. Patterns and suggestions for the lion.

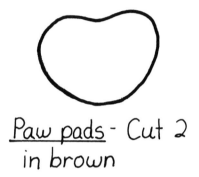

Paw pads - Cut 2
in brown

Toe pads - Cut 8
in brown

Tail - Cut 1

Fig. 3.51. Stitch yarn to the lion's head between and in front of ears.

Fig. 3.52. Continue adding yarn down the lion's face and under the chin.

Fig. 3.53. Stitch the next row approximately ¼ inch behind the first. Loose ends point toward the face while yarn is stitched, then are flipped back away from the face when mane is finished.

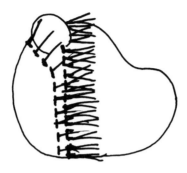

Fig. 3.54. Stitch rows of yarn to the back of the head in a circular pattern, then flip yarn down into place and comb with fingers.

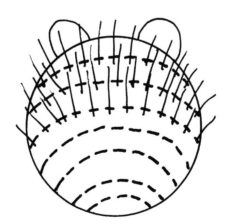

Wolf: Steps in Applying Facial Trim

1. Pin all pieces into place before gluing or sewing. Refer to figure 3.41 for placement.

2. Glue or sew the following pieces into place in the order given:

   tongue
   teeth
   yellow eye piece
   brown eye piece
   black pupil
   eyebrows

3. Sew two ear pieces together, right sides out, for each ear. Sew ears onto top of head by hand.

4. The next step involves the large pieces labeled "fur trim for head" (figure 3.42). Applying one piece at a time, start at the tongue and place along the top edge of teeth. Sew this narrow section onto the sock along the top and bottom edges, as in figure 3.43. Then cover back of head with the large portion, overlapping at the back and stretching the fabric up to the back of the ears and down to the finger opening. Glue into place onto the head. At the overlapped edge along the back of the head, trim where necessary to create a neat line.

5. Sew a 1½-inch button into place for a nose.

Bear: Steps in Applying Facial Trim

1. Pin all pieces into place before gluing or sewing. Refer to figure 3.44 for placement.

2. Glue a 1½-inch pompom slightly below center of face for a muzzle.

3. Sew two ear pieces together, right sides out, for each ear. Sew the ears onto the top of the head, slightly to each side of the head.

4. Sew on the covering for the back of the head, bringing the V-shaped cutout edges together at the neck area (see figure 3.46).

5. Sew on the covering for the top of the head, bringing the V-shaped cutout edges together, slightly overlapping the top piece over the back piece (see figure 3.47).

6. Sew on trim close to the ears, making sure it meets the edges of the other trim at the sides of the face. Refer to figure 3.48 for detail.

7. Sew three 9/16-inch dark brown buttons into place for eyes and, centered on pompom, nose.

Lion: Steps in Applying Facial Trim and Mane

1. Pin all facial pieces into place before gluing or sewing. See figure 3.49.

2. Sew two ear pieces together, right sides out, for each ear. Sew the ears into place on the head by hand.

3. Glue or sew the following pieces into place in the following order:

    > green eye pieces
    > black pupils (sew over green pieces)
    > eyelids (overlap top of eyes)
    > tongue
    > mouth (slightly overlap tongue)
    > nose (slightly overlap mouth with felt nose, or use a black button)

4. Cut at least sixteen pieces of yarn, each approximately 7 inches long. Place the yarn pieces side by side between the lion's ears, alternating colors, as shown in figure 3.51. Stitch along the center of the yarn pieces, fastening the yarn to the sock with small, tight stitches. Continue cutting lengths of yarn, placing and sewing them in front of the ears. Flip both ends of the yarn forward toward the face. Continue adding yarn down the sides of the face and under the chin (figure 3.52). Flip these pieces back away from the face. This completes the first two rows of yarn.

5. To create the rest of the mane, place 4½-inch pieces of yarn approximately ¼ inch behind the first row of yarn and behind the ears, as shown in figure 3.53. This row goes down the sides of the face but not under the chin. Stitch into place with tight stitches on the sock. Repeat with as many rows as needed to cover the head, in a circular pattern, as in figure 3.54, with the rows growing smaller and smaller. Flip all rows back and down away from the face to create a fluffy, full look. Trim the mane where necessary. Do not trim all the pieces of yarn evenly. Ends of varying lengths will result in a more natural look. Many pieces of yarn and numerous stitches are required to create a full mane. The puppet maker who does not skimp here will end up with a lion with a thick, furry mane that will delight the audience as well as the maker.

4

Stages, Scenery, and Props

Just as there exists a variety of types of puppets, so too is there a wide range of puppet stages. The basic requirements for puppetry instructors to keep in mind are that the stage should be simple to use, sturdy, and the proper width and height for comfortable use by the puppeteers. Stages may be portable or permanently located. Portable stages must be lightweight and either foldable or easy to assemble and take apart. Sturdiness is important. A stage that wiggles from side to side with the puppeteers' movement is distracting to the audience. A stage that is too lightweight and improperly balanced might even tip over. The people in the first row of an audience should not have to worry about a stage falling on them!

TYPES OF STAGES

In most stages, the puppet operators will either sit or stand behind and below the top of the stage front and hold the puppet up above their heads, or they will sit or stand behind a curtain with the puppet extended in front of the curtain (see figures 4.1 and 4.2).

Fig. 4.1. Puppeteer stands behind and below top of stage front

Fig. 4.2. Puppeteer stands behind curtain with puppet in front of curtain.

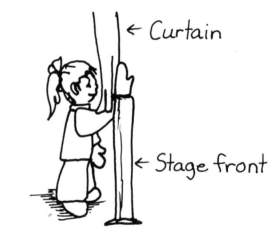

Curtain

The best type of curtain is one that will hide the puppeteers from the audience but will allow the puppeteers to see what they are doing. If the puppet operators are standing in front of a background curtain, as in figure 4.1, the curtain may be almost any type of fabric. But if the puppeteers must see through the fabric, a scrim curtain is recommended. A scrim is a gauzelike curtain, which when lit from the front allows the performers to see their puppets but keeps the puppeteers hidden. Actual scrim is an expensive fabric available only through theatrical supply houses. Any black, gauzelike fabric may be used for a scrim curtain.

Simple Stages to Make

An extremely simple and portable stage consists of a curtain hung from a tension-type curtain rod (figure 4.3). This is very portable and may be used in a doorway or between bookcases in a library. The height of the rod may be adjusted to the height of the puppeteers, who sit or stand behind the curtain. If this type of stage is used between bookcases, a background curtain may be placed behind and above the front curtain (see figure 4.4). This type of stage works best with a small number of puppeteers.

Fig. 4.3. A curtain hung from a tension rod provides a simple portable stage.

Fig. 4.4. A second curtain hung behind and higher than the front curtain provides a backdrop.

 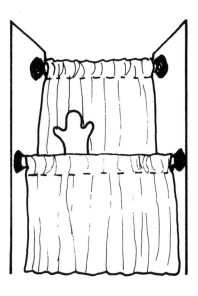

A large piece of corrugated cardboard will work as a stage, although it will not be as long lasting or as sturdy as other stages (figure 4.5). If a tabletop stage is desired, a piece of cardboard approximately 20 inches high may be placed on a table and a sheet or curtain fabric attached to the table to hide the legs of the puppeteers.

Fig. 4.5. A simple corrugated cardboard stage. A shorter stage may be used on a tabletop.

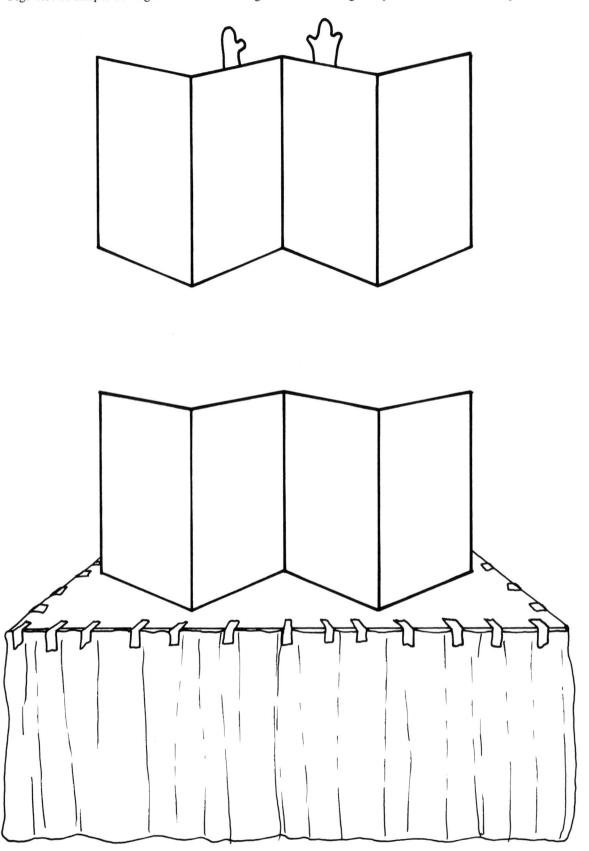

An easily constructed stage that would be sturdier can be made from three pieces of wooden paneling or plywood, hinged together as shown in figure 4.6. The front section should be 7 to 10 feet wide. A height of 36 to 39 inches should allow the puppeteers to sit on stools or kneel behind the stage and hold the puppets above their heads. If a background curtain is desired, a 1-by-2-inch board may be nailed or screwed to the end of each side section. The boards should be 18 to 24 inches higher than the stage, with a hole drilled into each near the top. A dowel rod will fit through the holes, and a background curtain may be hung from the rod (figure 4.7). A café-style curtain hung from rings works best if scenery posters are to be used, as detailed in the scenery section of this chapter.

A similar type of stage is shown in figure 4.8. The opening in the stage allows the puppet operators to sit behind a curtain and hold the puppets out in front of the curtain. This is less tiring for the arms than holding the puppets overhead. Notches near the front of each side section support a dowel rod from which the curtain hangs. In addition, a curtain rod may be screwed or nailed to the reverse side of the stage just above the opening. The stage curtain, in two sections, hangs from the curtain rod and is pushed apart for the performance and closed between scenes (figure 4.9). Or a window shade may be fastened above the opening to provide a "curtain" that may easily be raised and lowered.

(Text continues on page 85.)

Fig. 4.6. A hinged, three-section wooden stage.

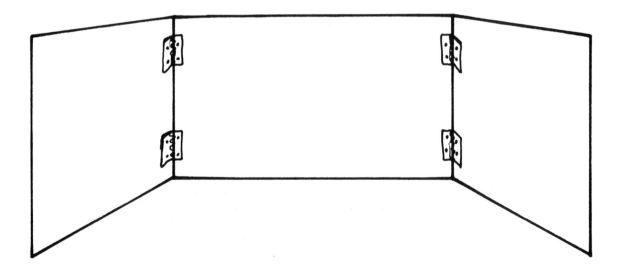

Fig. 4.7. Wooden stage with backdrop curtain hung from a dowel rod.

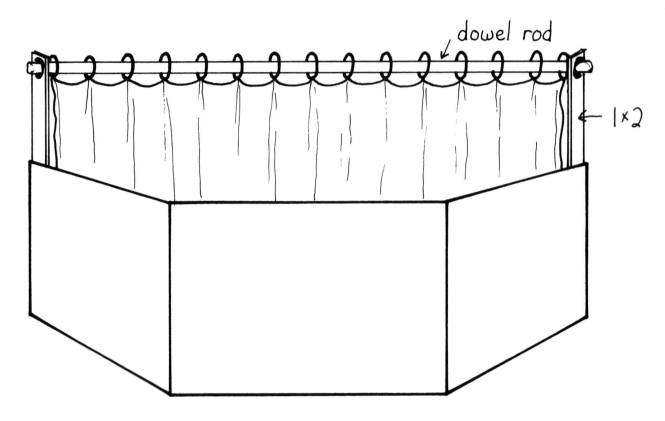

Fig. 4.8. Wooden stage with window for performance area.

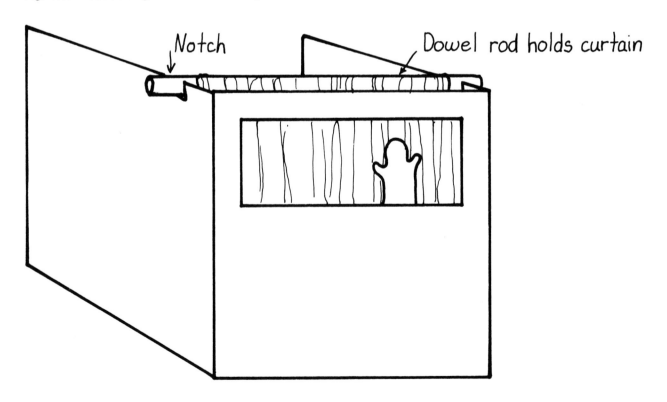

Fig. 4.9. A curtain rod may be fastened to the back of the stage above the window.

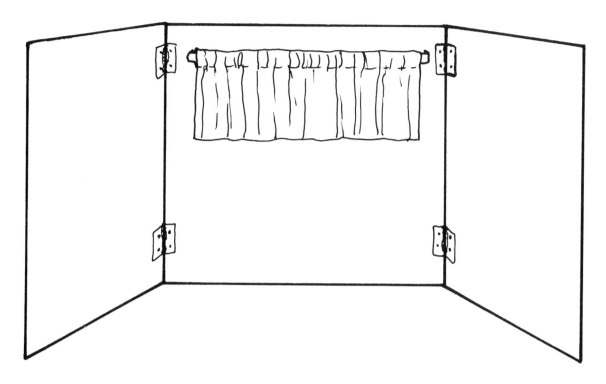

Sources for Plans and Instructions

The above stages are relatively easy to make. Other materials from which stages may be constructed include plastic PVC pipe and metal pipe. Readers who wish to see detailed plans for constructing puppet stages should consult the following books (see bibliography at the end of this book for full references):

Creegan, George. *Sir George's Book of Hand Puppetry.* Chicago: Follett, 1966.

Provides detailed instructions for a folding wooden frame stage and an aluminum frame stage with metal couplings.

Hanford, Robert Ten Eyck. *The Complete Book of Puppets and Puppeteering.* New York: Sterling, 1976.

Provides plans for a folding tabletop plywood stage.

Hawes, Bill. *The Puppet Book.* San Diego, Calif.: Beta Books, 1977.

Includes directions for a plywood stage as well as one made from PVC pipe, a lightweight plastic.

Renfro, Nancy. *A Puppet Corner in Every Library.* Austin, Tex.: Nancy Renfro Studios, 1978.

Gives instructions for making a variety of stages, from lap and tabletop models to more elaborate types.

Sources for Purchasing Puppet Stages

Professional-quality puppet stages may be purchased from the following sources:

Brodart Catalog
Eastern Division
   P.O. Box 3037
   1609 Memorial Avenue
   Williamsport, PA 17705

Western Division
   1236 S. Hatcher Street
   City of Industry, CA 91748
   1-800-223-8467

Nancy Renfro Studios
1117 W. 9th Street
Austin, TX 78703
1-800-933-5512
(512) 327-9588

Puppet Productions, Inc.
P.O. Box 82008
San Diego, CA 92138
(619) 565-2343

Professionally made puppet stages can be expensive. Thus, before purchasing one, it is wise to be sure the stage will meet the needs of the people who will be using it. It should stand at a height that is comfortable for the puppet operators to use. A width of 6 feet will provide enough room for three or four puppeteers to perform at the same time. When more people are needed to operate puppets at the same time, a width of 7 to 10 feet is best.

LIGHTING

Stage lights are not always necessary, but they do add a professional touch and can enhance the puppets and scenery. If stage lights are not used, the area near the stage must be well lit. A large room with separate controls for the front and back of the room allows performers to turn off the back lights while keeping the front of the room lit.

Lights are necessary when a scrim curtain is used. The lights will allow the performers to see their puppets while they, themselves, hide behind the curtain. Indoor flood lamps fitted into sockets with clamps (sold in hardware and photo stores) may be clamped to the front of the stage and aimed at the performance area. Or lights may be positioned on the floor in front of the stage and aimed upward toward the stage. If the lights are placed on the floor, any wires leading from them should be taped down to avoid the hazard of someone tripping over them in the semidarkness.

A stage may be equipped with fluorescent lights mounted with screws to the top of the stage. These may be ordinary household under-the-counter-type light fixtures, which may be purchased at hardware, lighting, and department stores. They should be aimed down toward the performance area. The raised stage curtain hides the lights so they do not shine into the audience's eyes.

MICROPHONE

If the audience is large, a microphone is necessary. It is frustrating for the audience to see the puppets but not be able to hear the performers. A portable microphone and speaker system works well. The microphone should be mounted backstage, to free the puppet operators from having to juggle it.

SCENERY

While scenery is not always essential to a puppet show, it does add to the mood and atmosphere of the story, and often it helps make clear to the audience where the action is taking place. In some cases the scenery is very important, as in "The Cat and Mouse in Partnership," where the action moves quickly from the house to the church. And with some scripts, the scenery is absolutely necessary, as in "Percy's Tale," or "Behind the Doors," in which two characters open several doors on their journey to save their friend.

Large and Clear

Whether used to enhance the script or used as an integral part of the story, scenery must be clear and easy for the audience to see. Tiny, detailed drawings will be lost to the audience. Large, bright scenery done with paint or markers will enhance the puppet show. The scenery makers need not worry that their backgrounds don't look realistic. Rather, the scenery should suggest the setting and help create a mood. A background should not be so busy that it competes with the puppets or the dialogue. A few large trees can suggest a forest; a throne and an arched doorway can give a sense of the grandeur of a palace.

To further enhance the mood and add interest, a three-dimensional effect can be achieved by attaching materials to the background. Bits of tinsel can add a festive touch, cotton can suggest snow, and red or orange cellophane can suggest a fire. In "The Forest Princess," silver foil may be used to suggest a waterfall, which is an important aspect of the final scene.

Suggestions for Quick and Easy Mounting of Scenery

It is vital that the scenery be easy and quick to put up and take down for scenery changes during the performance. A murmuring, squirming audience will result if people have to wait too long between scenes. There are many different methods of attaching scenery to the stage, and the type of stage will largely determine how this is to be done. The following are suggestions for methods of mounting scenery that allow for quick changes.

One method is to use paints or markers to create the background scenes on large pieces of posterboard. Punch two or three holes at the top of the boards and tie them to the top of the stage with fishing line or string (figure 4.10). Then just flip to the desired poster between scenes. The scenery hangs from the same bar as the background curtain; thus, a café-style curtain hung from rings works best. A stage without an overhead bar, such as that in figure 4.8, may have scenery hung from a dowel rod placed just in front of the background curtain (figure 4.11). If there is not enough room to flip posters over, each scene may be attached to a separate dowel rod. A dowel is lifted out of the groove and the next one set into place for a scene change.

An equally simple method is to paint the scenery on muslin and pin it to the background curtain with a straight pin at each corner. Large individual pieces of scenery, such as a table and chair or a house, may be painted on muslin and cut out or cut from colored felt and pinned onto the curtain instead of an entire scene.

Fig. 4.10. Scenery drawn on posterboards tied to the top of the stage may be flipped over for scene changes.

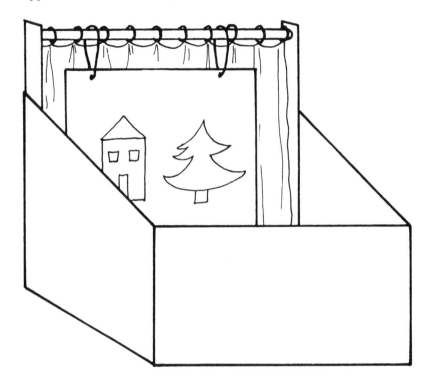

Fig. 4.11. Front dowel rod holds scenery. Rear dowel rod holds background curtain.

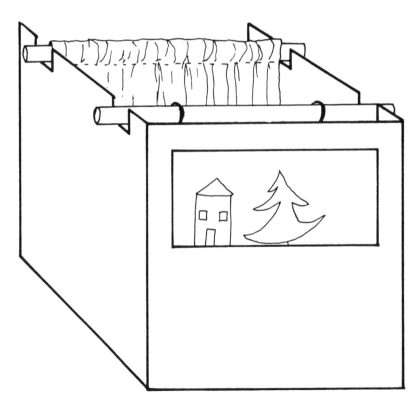

An easy way to use scenery with a corrugated cardboard stage is to draw individual items such as trees or houses onto sturdy posterboard or cardboard and cut them out. Then attach them to the reverse side of the stage with thumbtacks or pushpins (figure 4.12).

Fig. 4.12. Scenery pieces may be attached with thumbtacks or pushpins to a cardboard stage.

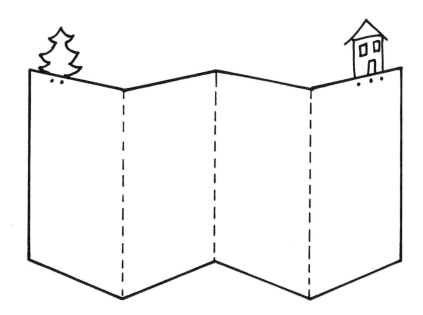

Another method is to mount pieces of scenery onto a board at the stage "floor" (where the puppets stand), at either side of the stage. Figure 4.13 shows a board with slots cut into it. Pieces of scenery mounted on sticks may be slid forward into place (figure 4.14). This is a good method to use when characters need to emerge from a house or hide behind a bush.

Fig. 4.13. 1-by-2-inch board with slots cut out is attached to stage.

Fig. 4.14. Scenery is slid forward in slot. A wooden pin, nail, or screw keeps the item at the proper height.

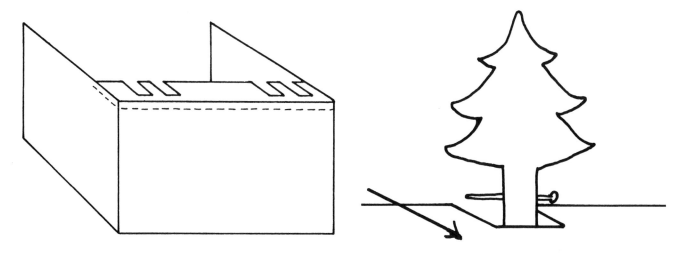

A similar method is to drill holes, rather than cut slots, into the board. The scenery pieces are mounted on dowel rods with a screw to keep them from falling too low (figure 4.15). This method works well with "Percy's Tale," allowing the doors to be pushed open by the characters.

Fig. 4.15. Holes may be drilled into a board to hold pieces of scenery.

PROPS

In addition to scenery, props will add visual interest to a puppet show and make the production more polished and professional looking. In some cases, props are necessary: the pot of fat in "The Cat and Mouse in Partnership"; the cape Bright Star wears as a disguise and the quilt with which she is covered in "Star Light, Star Bright"; and the rope and the book in "The Land of Rainbows." Care should be taken, however, not to go overboard with props. The puppeteers should know when to let the audience use their imaginations. For example, in a scene in which characters eat, they do not actually have to pick up silverware and food. Their movements and words will enable the audience to imagine that they are eating. Too many props can be distracting. And when puppeteers, especially beginners, have to worry about handling a large number of props, their performance may suffer as they pay less attention to their movements and the delivery of their lines. Realistic gestures and movements will help the audience fill in what is missing.

When props are used, they need to be large enough to be seen by the audience. This often means that a puppet will hold an object that is actually out of proportion to the puppet's body—for example, a book that is larger than one a character that size would read. This is to be expected if the audience is to see it.

Props must also be simple to use. The easiest props for a puppeteer to handle are items that can hang from a puppet's arm. The pot of fat in "The Cat and Mouse in Partnership" may be a pail with a handle that can be slipped over the cat's paw. And in "The Town Mouse and the Country Mouse," Lucinda's suitcase has a handle that is longer than a real suitcase handle. This also frees Lucinda's other hand for gestures such as pointing or waving about.

In addition to props that hang from a puppet's arm, some props may be fastened to the puppet with small pieces of hook and loop fasteners (Velcro™) sewn to the prop and to the puppet's hand. Props may also be held onto the puppet's hand with a rubber band. Of course, this method is not useful if a prop is to be passed from one character to another. If the passing of props is necessary, the puppet operators must practice the action over and over until they can do it with ease.

SPECIFIC SCENERY SUGGESTIONS

The following suggestions detail the scenery used in performances of four of the puppet shows for which scripts are provided in part III. Each of the shows was presented at the Lake Villa District Library in Lake Villa, Illinois.

"The Town Mouse and the Country Mouse"

Figures 4.16-4.17 show the scenery used for "The Town Mouse and the Country Mouse." Scenery was drawn on white posterboard and hung from the top of the stage, as in figure 4.10.

Fig. 4.16. Scenery from "The Town Mouse and the Country Mouse."

Fig. 4.17. Scenery from "The Town Mouse and the Country Mouse."

"Star Light, Star Bright"

The same type of scenery was made for "Star Light, Star Bright." Only two background scenes were required. The day scene was drawn on white posterboard and featured a large mountain, a tree, grass, and a light blue sky. For the night scenes, small stars were cut from foil paper and glued to a dark blue piece of posterboard. This basic night scene was used for scenes 1, 3, and 4. Large cardboard cutouts of Big Star, a tree, and Star Bright were attached with paper clips to the night sky scene in scenes 3 and 4.

"The Forest Princess"

This show featured simple pieces of scenery cut from paper and pinned to the background curtain (figure 4.18). The forest was represented by four trees and the throne room by the thrones of the king and

Fig. 4.18. Throne room from "The Forest Princess."

queen. The children trimmed the thrones with tinsel to enhance the grandeur of the palace. The waterfall was made from silver foil and surrounded by shrubbery made from crepe paper and real twigs and leaves.

"Percy's Tale," or "Behind the Doors"

"Percy's Tale" involved a more complicated scenery arrangement but one that held the audience in fascination. As in figure 4.15, six cardboard doors were fastened with a staple gun to dowel rods and slid into place in holes on a 1-by-2-inch wooden board. In part III, the script for "Percy's Tale" gives complete instructions for the use of the doors. Each door had a picture on the back to represent what the characters saw when they opened that door. The puppets opened a door by pressing on one side and giving it a 180-degree turn to reveal the reverse side. The puppeteer's hand below eye level of the audience helped control the turn of the door.

Scenery, though it should not overwhelm the puppets or be too cumbersome to use with ease, will add to the overall mood of the puppet show and to the enjoyment of the audience. Just as there are varied types of puppet stages, so too are there many ways to construct and mount scenery. Creating scenery will be one of the aspects of the workshop that the participants will enjoy and that will challenge the imaginations of both instructor and participants.

Part II
Running a Puppet Workshop for Children

Children and puppets go together—children in the audience, but also children as puppeteers. Part II provides instruction for running a workshop in which children are taught to make puppets, to use them skillfully, and to put on a puppet show for an audience. The instructor is taken through the steps, from the preliminary selection of script and planning for the workshop; through puppet and scenery construction, assignment of roles, and practice with puppets; through rehearsals; and finally through the performance itself. Workshop leaders, from novice to skilled, if well prepared, will bring the joy of puppetry to the children.

A magical world will be created as the puppets come to life and interact with each other on the stage. Parts I and II of this book provide the instructor with a complete plan for helping children learn to make and manipulate puppets and to create the magic of puppetry while they gain confidence and develop their creativity. Puppetry, then, is an ideal project for children and adults working together.

5

Beginning the Workshop

PRELIMINARIES

Deciding to hold a puppet workshop with children is just the first of many decisions an instructor must make. A number of things must be remembered before the first young puppeteer sets foot through the doorway.

The Workshop Participants

Two important considerations—and ones that will, in part, determine other decisions—are the number of participants and the age range of the children to be included. Schoolteachers working with one class or grade often will not have a choice here. If the workshop is a classroom activity, there may be thirty children of approximately the same age. But if the workshop is an optional after-school activity, or if it is offered at a public library or other place open to the public, the instructor needs to set limits on both the number of children and the age range. It is difficult to teach the puppet-making part of the workshop to children much younger than seven or eight without a number of adult helpers on hand. If a large number of children wish to participate, several sessions may be offered rather than trying to do it in one huge group. With ten to fifteen participants, there are usually enough children for two short puppet shows, or for one show with a larger cast plus children to operate lights, curtain, music, and scenery and to introduce and close the show. A teacher conducting a puppet workshop with an entire class will find that things will run smoothly if the class is divided into several groups, each with its own adult leader, recruited from parents or aides.

Workshop Details: A Time Frame

The next decisions that must be made are the length of the workshop and the dates, times, and places for the workshop and the performance. A set of daily plans will help the instructor determine how many days will be needed for the workshop. The instructor should make two or three puppets in advance to get a feel for the amount of work involved and should plan on devoting several sessions to puppet and scenery making and practice with puppet manipulation. Several more days need to be spent on rehearsals for the performance. A chart similar to the one in figure 5.1 may be useful in planning the workshop sessions.

Time and place for the workshop may be determined by the individual circumstances. A teacher could hold the workshop in a classroom during school hours or immediately after school; a librarian or youth group leader might choose Saturday mornings or late afternoons when the children are free to participate. The workshop should be held in an area that will allow both privacy to the children who are practicing

Fig. 5.1. Careful planning is essential. The instructor may wish to fill in a chart similar to this or develop one that fits the particular needs of the workshop.

Number of participants: 12
Age range: 9-14
Dates of workshop sessions: June 13, 15, 20, 22, 27, 29, July 6, 11
Time of workshop: 9:00 - 11:00 a.m.
Place for workshop: library meeting room
Date(s) of performance(s): July 12
Time(s) of performance(s): 1:00 and 3:00 p.m.
Place of performance: library meeting room
Title of play(s): The Forest Princess
Type of puppet to be made: Styrofoam head puppets
Number of helpers, if any: 2

Session 1:
- Read over script
- Discuss characters
- Additional reading, rotating parts
- Discuss jobs: scenery, lights, curtain, music, introduction and closing for show
- Look at stage, lights

Session 2:
- Practice exercises
- Discuss music selections
- Read for parts
- Publicity for performance

Session 3:
- Assign parts
- Read over script
- Puppet exercises
- Begin construction of puppets and scenery

Session 4:
- Choose music
- Puppet exercises
- Read over script
- Puppet and scenery construction

Session 5:
- Begin blocking while reading script at stage
- Puppet and scenery construction

Sessions 6-8:
- Rehearse with curtain, scenery, lights, music

and quiet to the other people in the building. A librarian, then, needs to reserve a separate room for the workshop, if at all possible, rather than use a corner of the main library. A library workshop may be held twice a week after school for four or five weeks. A note sent home with each participant after the first session should clearly list dates and times of all workshop sessions and the performance or performances.

The performance need not be presented in front of a large, formal audience. The show may be presented to younger children during one of the regularly scheduled library storyhours or, in a school, to children in other classes. Or the show may be a specially scheduled event to which children and parents are invited. Whatever the decision, it needs to be made in advance so the participants will know who their audience will be and when the performance will take place. If a room or auditorium must be reserved in a library, school, or church, this must be done in advance to avoid schedule conflicts and last-minute changes. The instructor also needs to decide whether publicity will be required to advertise the performance, if it is one to which the public is invited. Time may be set aside during the workshop to make posters or flyers.

The Stage

After it has been determined where the performance will take place, the instructor must take the time to become familiar with the stage or to construct a simple stage (see chapter 4). He or she needs to know how to operate the curtain as well as the sound and lighting systems, if there are any. It is a waste of valuable practice time if the instructor must figure out how to operate the curtain or lights while the children are waiting.

The Script

The next important decision is to select a script or scripts. As discussed in part III, children love interesting characters who do things and solve problems. They like suspense and humor.

When selecting a puppet play, the workshop leader needs to consider the number of children expected to participate. A group of fifteen children and a cast of only four characters don't match up. Also to be considered are the ages of the participants and the audience, the ease with which scenery and props can be made and utilized (too many scene changes disrupt the flow of the performance), and the size of the available stage. It simply may not be possible to use a play with a large cast in which all the characters appear onstage at the same time. That usually results in a lot of pushing, shoving, and bruised toes backstage.

When reading over possible scripts, the instructor should keep in mind flexibility in parts assignment. A script that includes several small parts with only a few lines provides some flexibility: If one performer quits or becomes ill, another performer with only a small part may take over the role. Due to an outbreak of flu, one library workshop that started with ten children practicing "The Forest Princess" ended up with six performers. The show went on, and the six children were able to handle the nine parts with no trouble, although the instructor had to jump in to do music and lights.

The instructor must make enough copies of the script for all the participants, plus a few to replace those that inevitably will be misplaced or left at home. The scripts should not be stapled together, as they will be easier to handle if the pages separate readily.

If time allows, a workshop leader may have the children write their own short scripts, based on familiar fairy tales or fables. Here, as with the puppet making, extra adults are handy. One adult working with each group will move things along and keep the children on task. Copies of the script must be made for each child in the group. Very young children may wish to present short nursery rhymes, either singly or in small groups.

Type of Puppet and Assembly of Materials

The choice of the script, the ages and abilities of the workshop participants, and the amount of time available will all help the instructor determine the type of puppet to be made and used for the performance. Part I provides patterns and ideas for simple stick puppets and felt puppets, as well as more involved Styrofoam-head hand puppets. Once the type of puppet has been determined, the workshop leader needs to assemble a variety of materials for the construction of the puppets. The leader may begin by looking through any materials and trims collected in the past. Let the public know that donations of fabric and trim are welcome. It may be wise to put out a list of specific items needed, such as eyelet lace, fake fur, yarn, buttons, and sewing needles. This helps the instructor avoid the task of wading through a mountain of unneeded material. There will always be items that have to be purchased, usually enough fake fur for the animals' bodies, craft glue, and yarn, paint, and felt in specific colors. Some of the fabrics may be found at reduced cost on remnant tables. Watch for sales and buy basic colors in advance. And some stores will donate remnants and leftover buttons to schools, libraries, and youth groups.

Materials also need to be assembled for the construction of the scenery, props, and, if necessary, publicity posters. These materials are detailed in part I. Items such as sewing machines, scissors, and needles for hand sewing must be obtained. One method of obtaining the latter two items is to request that each participant bring them to the workshop.

If each participant is to make his or her own puppet body, the availability of several sewing machines will help the process go quickly. A more practical method is to make the puppets in assembly-line fashion, with an older child or an adult helper sewing the bodies. The bodies and heads may be made in the assembly line; then each child may trim and finish the costume and facial features of his or her own puppet. Or the instructor may wish to sew the puppet bodies in advance and have the children make the heads and finish the puppets. Regardless of the method used, this is a decision that must be made before the workshop begins.

If adult helpers are desired for the puppet-making sessions, the instructor should arrange for their help in advance and get a firm commitment for the dates on which they are needed. One good source for helpers is the parents of the workshop participants.

Assignment of Parts

Another decision the leader must make is how to assign character parts. A beginning workshop leader may make the mistake of thinking that each child will want a different role in the play. That is rarely the case. Rather, there always seems to be one part—often the lead or a villain—that six or seven children want, and one part—a maid or the narrator—that no one wants. If the instructor does not make it clear from the beginning how the parts will be assigned, fighting among the participants and hurt feelings may result, and children may drop out of the workshop because of it.

The instructor may simply announce in advance that the names of all the people who want a particular part will be placed in a hat and one name will be drawn. That is a simple way to solve the problem. But another method may result in a more effective performance: The children are given a chance to practice all the lines individually or in small groups. The script is read over several times with the children rotating the parts. Characters are discussed. The scripts are taken home for more practice. Then, during the second or third session, the children read for the parts. It takes some of the pressure off the instructor if a committee composed of several teachers, librarians, or other adults assigns parts. The results are announced at the end of that session or at the beginning of the next one.

The workshop leader, then, must make a number of decisions and do some preliminary work to ensure a smoothly run workshop. The leader should keep in mind that the primary goal of the workshop is the enjoyment of the participants. It should not be expected that the performance will be a professional one. The children should have fun as they learn to make and manipulate puppets. With this in mind, and with the preliminary work done, the instructor is now ready for the children to arrive and for the workshop to begin.

THE WORKSHOP BEGINS

To encourage a relaxed atmosphere and enjoyment for everyone involved, the children should be given time to get to know each other and feel comfortable with each other from the beginning of the workshop. If the children are not already acquainted, nametags may be supplied, and the instructor should wear one as well. The children should be seated around a large table or on chairs arranged in a circle so that they can see and speak with one another.

Discusson of Roles

The workshop leader may wish to begin the first session with a discussion of the various roles to be filled. The puppeteers are not the only people necessary for a puppet play production. The leader should discuss the jobs of those who operate scenery, music, lights, and the curtain. It is also a good idea to have someone to introduce the play and to close the show by bidding the audience good-bye. This general narrator is very important and can set the tone for the entire production.

Discussion of Script

Next, the script may be presented and read through, with the children reading the various parts. If the children will be writing short scripts based on fairy tales, these stories should be discussed. In either case, the characters and plot should be discussed. Questions may be posed to generate discussion:

- Who is the protagonist (the one with whom the audience will side)? What are his or her main characteristics? Pick out some examples of words or actions that clearly reveal these traits.

- Who is the antagonist (the villain, or the one who poses a problem for or threat to the protagonist)? What are his or her main characteristics? Give examples of words and actions.

- What is the main problem in the story?

- How is this problem solved?

- How are the other characters important? What are the main traits of each of these characters?

- Which character or characters learn something during the play? What do they learn?

- What is the setting of the story? Where does each scene take place?

The first session may continue with another reading of the script, with the children switching parts. The child who read the main character's role in the initial reading may read a small part in the first scene, sit out scene 2, and read another part in a later scene, as the parts are rotated, to give everyone a feel for the various roles. Or the session may continue with groups of children beginning to write their own scripts.

Next, the leader needs to find out which children are interested in the various parts and which, if any, would rather work lights, music, scenery, and the curtain. The children should be reminded that those with smaller parts may also be called upon to do one of these backstage jobs.

Conclusion of First Session

The leader may conclude the first session by showing the children the puppet stage and by giving a quick lesson on the working of the lights and curtain. How the scenery is attached to the stage and changed between scenes should be demonstrated. The children may be allowed to practice raising and lowering the curtain. Children, especially those who have never been involved in a puppet production, are fascinated by these backstage workings, and the session ends with an air of excitement as they anticipate using the curtains and lights in the performance.

The children should be allowed to take home the scripts and should be reminded that during the next session they will be reading for the parts they desire.

THE NEXT SESSIONS

Session two usually begins with feelings of excitement and nervousness as the children discuss the parts they hope to get. They should be reminded that even if they do not play the lead, all participants are very important and that the performance will depend on everyone doing the best they can at their particular jobs. If writing their own scripts, children will need part of the second session for writing.

Exercise with Puppets

Before the readings begin, it is nice to loosen up the children with some general puppet practice exercises. Previously made puppets may be supplied for the children to use. If no such puppets are available, a sock with holes cut for the thumb and little finger, or a glove, will work just as well. Using the practice exercises provided in the following chapter, the instructor should have the children practice conveying emotions and actions through the movements and posture of their puppets. Emotions such as fear, surprise, joy, and sorrow, and actions such as walking, running, picking up an object, and pointing may be practiced. Chapter 6 gives specific exercises that will help the children develop realistic movements with puppets.

Music

The instructor may wish to devote part of session two to a discussion of the music that may enhance the show. He or she may wish to play portions of records or cassettes with music appropriate for the entrance of the hero or heroine or the villain. The hero or heroine's music may be joyful or dashing or may have a light feeling. The music for the villain may invoke an evil or menacing atmosphere. A scene may be introduced by a portion of a song with a quiet, pastoral feeling or a jazzy, busy sound.

The children will often volunteer their own suggestions for music. The leader should remind them that some music is protected by a copyright, but older pieces are in the public domain and are readily found on records and cassettes in the library. Some children may volunteer to look for and bring in pieces of music appropriate to the script for entrances of characters, for use during scene changes, or to open and close the show.

After final selection, the music must be carefully recorded onto a cassette tape. There will not be time during the performance to search for a particular portion of music. Rather, each piece must be recorded, in order, as many times as it will be used. A chart that lists each music selection and when to play it is helpful. A sample music chart for "The Town Mouse and the Country Mouse" may look like the one in figure 5.2. Thus, for "The Town Mouse and the Country Mouse" the peaceful music selection must be recorded onto the tape four times and the jazzy music twice, in the proper order. After recording the music, the instructor should listen to it carefully, while following the script, to be sure a selection has not been left out or incorrectly placed.

Publicity

After a discussion of the music, the instructor may bring up the idea of publicity for the performance. Participants should be encouraged to think of ideas for posters or flyers. They should be reminded that while some children are making scenery, others may be making posters or other publicity material.

Reading for the Parts

When it is time for the readings, any child who wants a part should be allowed to read. If the number of characters in a particular script simply is not enough for the number of participants, two or three of the children may be used in a short skit to introduce the play. Or nursery rhymes or short fairy tales might be presented before the play, much the way movie theaters used to run cartoons before the main attraction. It's fun to let the children who will be in these short skits decide on the puppet characters needed and even write the skits themselves.

Practice and Construction

During the next few sessions, the children will be involved in three primary activities. They should read through the script at least once during each session, with each participant reading his or her assigned part. They will construct puppets, scenery, and props. And they should continue to do some of the practice exercises as they learn to effectively manipulate puppets.

Two to three sessions should be allowed for the construction of puppets and scenery. The instructor should be familiar with the procedures detailed in part I, including the need to supply puppet patterns precut to save time. The instructor should also remember to allow the children to be creative, emphasizing that they do not need to stick to the drawings or photos of puppets in this book or in other examples. The

Fig. 5.2. Sample music chart for "The Town Mouse and the Country Mouse."

Purpose	Where in Script	Type of Music	Title
Introduction	After curtain is raised, before narrator speaks	Peaceful	
Scene change	Between scenes 1 and 2	Peaceful	
Scene change	Between scenes 2 and 3	Jazzy	
Scene change	Between scenes 3 and 4	Jazzy	
Chase music	Center p.7 script, where indicated in scene 4	The chase, fast	
Scene change	Between scenes 4 and 5	Peaceful	
Close of show	As final curtain falls	Peaceful	

children should be reminded to make costumes and facial features that emphasize the characters' personalities, and plenty of fabric and trim should be provided. Children may work in pairs on a puppet if there are more participants than puppets (figure 5.3).

Fig. 5.3. Children construct felt puppets during a workshop at the Lake Villa District Library.

Some children will want to make the scenery. As detailed in chapter 4, this should be kept simple: a few trees to suggest a forest, a throne and an arched doorway to suggest a castle, a table and chairs to suggest a kitchen.

Once these beginning steps are completed—the assigning of parts, practice exercises, discussion of music, and puppet and scenery construction—the participants will be ready to block the scenes (plan the placement and movement of the characters on the stage) and begin rehearsals.

6

Practice and Performance

A skilled puppeteer brings a puppet to life. The puppeteer's voice and movements transform the puppet from a piece of cloth into a character that seems to live and breathe on its own. Beginning puppeteers must therefore think carefully about the movements and voices they will use and take the time to practice them. Hand placement inside the puppets and basic manipulation of each type of puppet are covered in part I. In this chapter, specific exercises are provided for practice sessions with puppets.

PUPPET MOVEMENT

A puppet is relatively small and must be viewed by a large number of people in the audience. Sometimes it helps to exaggerate the movements. For example, to indicate that a puppet is trying to hear another puppet, the puppeteer may make the puppet's entire body lean toward the other character. To indicate surprise, the puppet may jump backward. A puppet may shake its entire body from side to side to indicate "No!" rather than merely turn its head. This requires a definite wrist-twisting motion by the puppeteer.

A puppet that is digging a hole may have to bend low at first and then raise its body until its hands are above and slightly behind its head. This, too, requires wrist movement rather than just finger movement. In this way, the audience will see the digging action much more clearly than if only the puppet's arms are moved up and down.

Specific Movements for Hand Puppet Practice

These movements may be practiced without dialogue. The actions must be clear and distinct.

1. Practice having a puppet pick up an object (real or imaginary). The movement must be deliberate: Extend puppet's arm forward, then make puppet bend over, pause, and raise body and arm. This is much more effective than merely having a puppet make a vague sweep at the stage floor.

2. Practice walking puppet. Hand puppets rarely have movable feet. So use short bounces to convey the idea of stepping.

3. Practice running. Use taller, quicker bounces. Do not merely whiz the puppet across the stage.

4. To make a puppet point at something, move your wrist to turn the puppet slightly while extending one of the puppet's arms.

5. Have the puppet pull a heavy object across the stage. A puppet that leans forward as it slowly moves ahead will appear to be straining under the weight.

6. To indicate a chase, the puppet being chased should run onto the stage with tall, quick bounces, looking over a shoulder from time to time.

7. Waking up may be shown by starting with a puppet lying down. Have the puppet stretch its arms upward and rub its eyes before it slowly stands up.

8. To show a character sneaking onto stage, have the puppet walk slightly bent over and very slowly. It may move its head slowly to look around.

9. Have your puppet watch a bird or airplane flying overhead. Actions include looking up and turning the head slowly from one side to another, leaning back, and pointing. Be sure to have the puppet's eyes pointing in the proper direction: up at the imaginary object, not down, offstage, or at the audience.

Conveying Emotions

The words the characters speak will be enhanced if their actions match their moods. Practice conveying the following emotions without words. Workshop leaders and participants may develop additional actions with which to show these feelings.

1. Anger: shake fist; shake head.

2. Sorrow: place hands on both sides of head while shaking head from side to side, or cry with head bent and hands held to eyes.

3. Joy: clap hands, jump up and down. (Remember, stick, felt, or Styrofoam head puppets cannot smile!)

4. Shyness: turn away from front of stage, bow head. Back up.

5. Fear: quiver, back up, hold hands out in front of body.

6. A haughty attitude: point to self, nose in air.

7. Evil intentions: rub hands together.

THE PUPPET'S VOICE

After practicing gestures and emotions, the puppeteer must think about how the puppet will speak. Words must be spoken distinctly and loudly, but care must be taken to avoid yelling to be heard by the audience. It is essential to practice speaking aloud while moving the puppet.

It is the puppeteer's job to make the puppet believable. Both the voice and the actions used by the puppeteer must be consistent with the personality of the character. The tone of voice must match the character's mood. The age and type of character must be considered. A high, squeaky voice is appropriate for a young mouse but not for a middle-aged king. An excitable or fearful character may speak rapidly, whereas a sneaky villain may quietly and slowly reveal his thoughts. The puppeteer may have to try several voices aloud in practice before finding the type of voice that is consistent with the puppet's personality.

Foreign accents should be used with care and only if essential to the meaning of the character. Beginning puppeteers who try accents are difficult to understand—and the accent frequently comes and goes during the puppet show, which can be very confusing to the audience.

The voices of the puppets must be different from each other to help the audience distinguish between the characters on stage. This is especially important if one person is operating more than one puppet. Again, practicing aloud is the way to ensure that the voices remain distinct. Puppeteers should strive to make each character a unique and lively creation. There should be no boring puppets! Whether a character is calm, excited, timid, joyful, or mean, the puppeteer must give it life!

One way to give life to a puppet is to put action with the words. Movements can be used to emphasize specific words:

"Stay away from me!"—Puppet may push another puppet away while saying *away*.

"I won't do it!"—Shake head on *won't*.

"I won't do it."—Point to self on *I*.

"What was that?"—Look up or off to side on *that*.

Simple movements such as waving, pointing, and shaking the head enhance the meaning of the spoken words. However, this doesn't mean that the puppets should bounce all around the stage in frenzied activity. Every movement should contribute to the meaning. Unnecessary movement is confusing to the audience.

PUPPET INTERACTION

Voice and actions are particularly important when characters interact onstage. Care must be taken to hold the puppets at the correct height in relation to each other. A little girl should not appear to be taller than her father. Puppets need to be face-to-face when addressing one another. It is very confusing to the audience when one puppet speaks to another but is facing the audience, another character, or even the back curtain! (This does happen sometimes when puppeteers don't watch their puppets during practice.) If more than two characters are onstage, the one who is speaking must turn toward the one being addressed. The speaking character should use actions appropriate to the dialogue while the rest of the characters freeze. This way, the audience can tell which one is speaking. The listening puppets should stand in as natural a position as possible, leaning toward the speaker if the intention is to convey intense listening or difficulty in hearing the speaker. The listeners may react subtly when it will enhance the dialogue—for example, stepping back in disgust or fear or shaking a head in sorrow immediately after the speaker has delivered a line.

Puppeteers need to practice together to synchronize their movements. The puppets' hands must meet when they shake hands, or each will appear to be shaking the air. When one puppet hands an object to another, the second puppet needs to reach out to take it. If one must pat another on the back, the other must be close enough to allow that action. When one character scares another, the other must jump and gasp. If one puppet chases and catches another, the other must stop running and allow itself to be caught.

EXERCISES FOR PRACTICE IN A
WORKSHOP SETTING

It is a good idea to arrange the group in a circle so the members may watch each other's puppets. At home, practicing in front of a mirror is a valuable technique.

1. One at a time, without words, perform an action to convey one of the following emotions. The others in the group will guess what the emotion is.

joy	timidity	anger
surprise	relief	sorrow
fear	meanness	

2. Have your puppet perform the following actions:

- Run, fall, get up, and brush off dirt.

- Watch something high in the sky (an airplane, bird, or baseball in flight).

- Knock on a door. React to who answers in joy, surprise, or fear.

- Eat and drink.

- Look for something. Find it.

- Run as if being chased.

- Think hard; then get an idea.

- Fall asleep.

- Wake up.

- Sweep.

- Cook.

- Bow.

- Dig a hole.

- Sneak onto stage and look around.

- Pull something heavy.

3. Exercises for two people: Improvise words to go with the actions. Be sure the audience can tell which puppet is speaking.

   - One character comforts the other.

   - One chases the other.

   - One tells the other a secret.

   - One tells the other exciting news.

   - One hands an imaginary object to the other.

   - One is angry with the other. The other is sorry.

   - One wants to play, but the other is shy.

   - One sings off key; the other cringes.

   - One is old, the other young. They both walk and then sit down. (There should be a contrast in the type of movements used.)

   - Two characters argue about where to go next.

   - Two characters hug because they have made up after an argument.

4. Perform appropriate action while saying the following. Practice performing the action while saying different words to change the emphasis. (For example, in the first statement, emphasize *I* then *won't* then *that*.

   - I won't do that!

   - Was that thunder?

   - I found it!

   - You'll never get away from me!

   - Leave me alone!

   - I'm so beautiful!

   - Hurry up! Hurry up!

   - It is cold in here!

   - It is so hot in here!

- I'm so tired.

- What a beautiful view!

- I can't find it anywhere.

- I think we're lost.

- It's OK. I forgive you.

- You don't really mean that, do you?

REHEARSAL

After some work with the practice exercises, it is time to rehearse the show. This is a time of excitement in the workshop; some of the participants may already have inquired more than once, "When do we get to start doing the show?"

Several rehearsals will be necessary before things run smoothly. This is a time to identify and solve the problems that may come up as the participants adjust to their roles both onstage and offstage.

Blocking the Scenes

The first rehearsal is usually a long one, because each scene must be blocked. Blocking involves the placement and movement of the characters on stage. Puppeteers must know their positions behind the stage for each scene and must know where the puppets will enter, exit, and move while on stage. They must know the direction their puppets will be facing while delivering the lines. Two phrases with which puppeteers should be familiar are "stage left" and "stage right." Stage left is the left-hand side of the stage from behind the curtain, from the puppeteer's viewpoint (see figure 6.1.) This appears as the right-hand side of the stage to the audience.

During the early rehearsals, then, the puppeteers practice getting their puppets on and off the stage and practice moving their puppets around the stage without bumping into each other. If a scene calls for two characters to embrace, the puppets must be close enough to do so. If two characters are to exit together, the puppets must face and move in the same direction without having to cross in front of other puppets. This helps avoid a tangle of arms behind the stage.

Posture

Attention must also be paid to the posture of the puppets onstage. Puppeteers may have to be reminded about the puppet exercises they have done. Puppets must not be allowed to dip behind the stage as a scene progresses and arms begin to tire. Puppets that lean outward toward the audience appear either to be lazy or to be talking to the audience rather than to each other. Puppets must be held straight and steady. If the script calls for a puppet to address the audience, then the puppet faces and leans toward the audience as it speaks. Otherwise, a puppet should face the character it is addressing.

Fig. 6.1. Puppet at stage left, seen from backstage; puppet at stage left seen from audience.

The director should check to see that the puppet that is speaking moves in an appropriate manner while the other puppets remain still; this avoids confusion about which character is speaking. The movements must coincide with the words the character is saying. "Look over there" should be accompanied by pointing or turning while the words are being said, not a beat or two later.

Voice

If only one problem will be evident from the beginning, it will most likely be volume. The puppeteers need to be reminded to speak loudly. One technique that brings good results is to tell puppeteers to speak more loudly than they think they need to speak. They may have to be reminded, "Use your outside voice," or, "Speak as loudly as if you are calling to your brother or sister outside." It will take some practice before the participants discover the dividing line between speaking loudly and yelling. The idea is not to have the puppets shouting at each other, but the people in the audience, including those in the back row, do need to hear the lines.

Often, in an effort to speak more loudly, a person will speak at a higher and higher pitch. A conscious effort must be made to keep the pitch consistent and natural while speaking loudly.

Volume is also affected by the direction in which a person speaks. Puppeteers must never speak down toward the floor. The curtain will somewhat muffle the voices; thus, sound must be projected up toward the puppets and over the curtain.

If a sound system is used during a performance for a large audience, the puppeteers must practice with it in order to know how loudly to speak. Care must be taken not to shout into the microphone.

In addition to volume, attention must be paid to the rate and clarity of speech. Speakers must not rush through their lines or allow their words to trail off at the ends of sentences. It may be necessary to have the puppeteers speak their lines over and over again before the desired levels of volume, rate, and clarity are established.

Scenery and Props

Rehearsals must include the use of scenery and props if these are to be used during the performance. Scenery changers and prop handlers must be designated and must know their responsibilities. Scenery and props must be easily and quickly put up and removed between scenes, as detailed in chapter 4. Props must be onstage when needed in order to avoid puppeteers fumbling for them behind stage. It is usually better to have one person responsible for all the props than to have individual puppeteers try to keep track of their props and puppets at the same time. The prop master may be a puppeteer with a small part in the show or may only handle props (or props and scenery) and not work a puppet.

Backstage Organization

The organization of puppets, props, and scripts backstage will help determine how smoothly the performance will run. Props should be in one place and always returned to that place. This may be a small table behind the puppeteers or a shelf or shelves attached to the stage (see figure 6.2.) If the scenery is not affixed to the stage but is to be put up and taken down, it should be neatly stacked on a separate table or against one of the sides of the stage. It may help to label the backs of the scenery pieces—for example, "Trees: Scenes 1, 3, 5, and 6." The scenery changer must keep the scenery in the proper order to avoid having to search for a particular piece between scenes.

Fig. 6.2. Script pages hang from hooks. They are removed and discarded on the script shelf or on the floor behind the puppeteers.

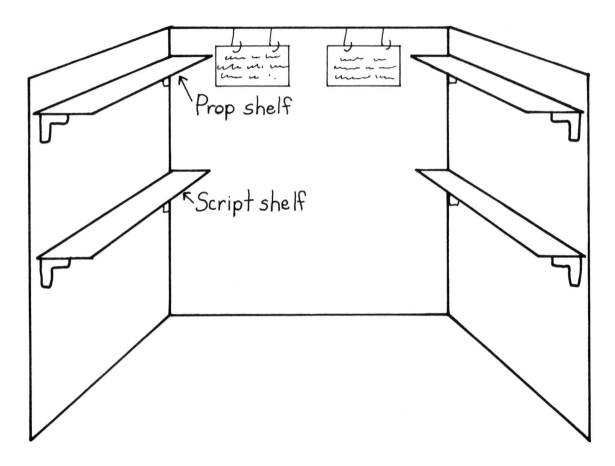

If the puppet show is not memorized, scripts may be held in the puppeteers' free hand or may be attached to the back of the stage near eye level. Puppeteers working more than one puppet at a time will need someone else to turn the pages. This must be worked out during rehearsals. Script pages may be taped individually to the back of the stage or hung from hooks; and as each page is finished, it is simply removed and set behind the puppeteers or on a shelf built for this purpose. (Refer again to figure 6.2.)

However the scripts are handled, the performers must practice handling the pages quietly. The sound of rustling pages from behind the stage will be distracting to the audience, as will whispering and giggling. Many performers have no idea how sounds carry from backstage to the audience; puppeteers who are allowed to watch some of the rehearsals can be made more aware of this.

Curtain and Music

Just as specific people must be designated to change scenery, others must be designated to raise and lower the curtain and to play any between-scene or background music. These people must also practice their jobs during rehearsal to ensure that things run smoothly and that everyone knows how much time will be required for these elements. Quick, smooth scene changes are accomplished only with practice and with cooperation among the puppeteers moving their puppets on and off the stage, scenery changers, prop master, curtain handler, and music master.

THE PERFORMANCE

Before the day of the puppet show, participants may take home a reminder note that invites parents and family members to the performance and that states the time the participants are to arrive. Puppeteers should arrive early enough to run through the show before the audience begins to arrive.

Welcome and Introduction

It is important that someone welcomes the audience and introduces the puppet show. This settles down the audience and perpares them to listen and watch. Puppet shows attract young children, and the instructor might address them in a friendly manner by asking if any of them have ever been to a puppet show. They may be reminded of the type of behavior required by the audience members (staying in their seats and avoiding talk during the show). They may be asked to suggest types of proper behavior, and their answers should be repeated for the entire audience to hear. Or a puppet may be used to carry on a conversation with the instructor in which the "rules" are revealed. This may be written out in advance by the leader or by the group as a whole during one of the workshop sessions.

After the short welcome, the puppet show itself is introduced. This may be done by the leader or by one of the workshop participants. The children themselves may plan and write the introduction. This should include announcing the title of the show and the name of the author. Each character may be introduced as the puppets take their places onstage.

The Show Goes On

Despite the discussion of proper audience behavior, there will probably be some noise from the audience. The puppeteers should try not to be distracted by it and should make every effort to speak loudly enough to be heard over it. At humorous points in a show, if the audience laughs (as is hoped they will), the puppeteers should briefly pause rather than allow the next line of dialogue to be lost in the laughter.

Puppeteers should remember that if they skip a word or misread a line during the performance, they should just go on rather than go back and try to correct it. If they drop a prop, it should be left alone if it cannot be retrieved easily and quickly by the puppet. A human hand appearing from behind the curtain to fetch a fallen object will break the spell of fantasy the puppets have created. The participants should realize that the performance may not be perfect. Maintaining a sense of humor will go a long way toward making it an enjoyable experience for the puppeteers and the audience.

Concluding the Show

Because the participants have worked hard during the workshop, they should be given some recognition when the performance is over. It's nice to call each one by name to appear in front of the curtain and take a bow. Some professional puppeteers feel that bringing the puppeteers out from behind the curtain spoils the magical spell of a puppet show by revealing that the puppets are not real. But these children are not professional puppeteers, and (let's face it) in most cases their parents have come to see them perform. They deserve some extra applause for their efforts, for the workshop has been a time of learning and hard work. Any script, curtain, and music handlers should also be called by name and should come out for their bows. Figure 6.3 shows some of the children, with their puppets, taking their bows after a performance.

Fig. 6.3. Children and puppets come out for a bow after a performance.

After the bows, the director or one of the children should thank the audience for attending and invite them back for future performances. This way, the members of the audience know that the show is over, and they are not wondering whether they should leave their seats or wait for something more.

As the workshop comes to an end and the puppets are taken home, the children who have participated in bringing them to life almost always ask when the next workshop will be. Any preperformance tension is gone, and they look forward to creating new puppets and staging another show. They will build on the knowledge they have acquired during this workshop, and the confidence they have gained will go with them into other facets of their lives. The performance is over, but the experience will remain with them, perhaps for a lifetime.

Part III
Eight Scripts for Puppet Shows

Interesting characters, lively action, and suspense—these are the elements that children of all ages enjoy, whether watching or performing in a puppet show. The following scripts contain such elements and are suitable for performance by children and young adults. The audience to which these plays are directed is children from approximately age four through junior high age. "The Cat and Mouse in Partnership" is an adaptation of a Grimms' fairy tale, "The Town Mouse and the Country Mouse" is from Aesop, and "The Smartest Person in the Village" is based on an old folktale. All are suitable for performance in a school, library, camp, or youth group setting.

The shows will encourage children to read and to use their imaginations. More important, though, are the delight and entertainment they will bring to the people who watch and are drawn into a land of make-believe, of fairy tales, of fun.

117

Star Light, Star Bright

PUPPET-MAKING NOTES:

Complete patterns and directions for making Star Bright, Big Star, and Gray Cloud are provided in chapter 1, figures 1.2-1.9. Complete patterns for the lion, mouse, reindeer, and Wendy are in chapter 2, figures 2.11 and 2.16-2.18.

CHARACTERS:
Narrator
Big Star (yellow star with top hat and bow tie)
Star Bright (yellow felt star with bow in hair)
Lion
Mouse
Reindeer
Wendy
Gray Cloud (gray cloud with frown and lightning bolt)

SCENERY: See "Specific Scenery Suggestions" in chapter 4.
Night sky with small stars
Day scene with mountain and tree
Night with Big Star in sky and tree in foreground
Night sky with small stars and Star Bright

MUSIC:
Opening music with star theme, such as "Twinkle, Twinkle, Little Star"
Sinister music for Gray Cloud
Closing music with star theme

PROPS:
Cape for Star Bright
Small quilt to cover Star Bright
Flashlight

SCENE 1:   Night sky with small stars

[Enter Narrator *as opening music plays]*

NARRATOR: Once upon a time there were many stars shining in the sky, much the way they shine now. But the two most important stars were Star Bright and Big Star.

[Enter Star Bright *and* Big Star *from opposite sides, facing away from each other]*

NARRATOR: Everything was fine in the heavens until one evening.... *[Exit* Narrator]

BIG STAR: Star Bright, oh, Star Bright, where are you? It's almost dark!

119

STAR BRIGHT: I'm not going to do it any more!

                       [Star Bright and Big Star turn to face each other.]

BIG STAR: What?

STAR BRIGHT: I'm done, finished, over—I resign!

BIG STAR: You what?

STAR BRIGHT: I quit!

BIG STAR: Star Bright, what are you talking about?

STAR BRIGHT: I'm not going to shine any more!

BIG STAR: But you're the evening star. You have to shine so children may make wishes on you.

STAR BRIGHT: I'm tired of granting wishes.

BIG STAR: Why?

STAR BRIGHT: Because so many people make such selfish wishes. People wish to be more beautiful or more rich, or to have more toys or more clothes. I'm beginning to think everyone on earth is selfish. I'm tired of it!

BIG STAR: Now, now, don't be silly. You have to shine in the sky and grant wishes.

STAR BRIGHT: No, I don't. I made my own wish. I wished that I could have a vacation. And I granted my own wish. I'm not shining tonight.

BIG STAR: Then what will you do?

STAR BRIGHT: I'm going to earth. I'm going to see if I can find one really nice person who isn't selfish. And I won't come back until I do!

BIG STAR: Well.... I can see how much you want to go. But the children will be disappointed if there's no star for them to wish upon tonight. *[Pause]* OK. I will shine in your place. But only for one night.

STAR BRIGHT: But it might take longer than one night for me to find someone who is really kind and unselfish.

BIG STAR:	One night! That is all. *[Pause]* Now, one more thing. This is important! There is a big gray cloud out there who likes to catch little stars and put out their lights. And he'd especially like to put out your light, Star Bright!
STAR BRIGHT:	I'll be careful.
BIG STAR:	I hope so! If something happens to you, no one will be able to wish on the evening star again.
STAR BRIGHT:	While I'm on earth, I don't want anyone to know I'm a star, so I'll have to disguise myself.
BIG STAR:	Good idea, but remember: Gray Cloud will be able to see right through your disguise. Watch out for him!
STAR BRIGHT:	I will. Good-bye, Big Star.
BIG STAR:	Good-bye, Star Bright.
	[Curtain]
SCENE 2:	Day scene with mountain and tree
	[Onstage: Star Bright, *wearing cape, standing near tree; enter* Mouse, *chased by* Lion*]*
LION:	*[Menacing voice]* When I see the first star tonight, I'm going to wish to finally catch you, little mouse! I'll wish I catch you and a dozen more like you!
MOUSE:	*[Squeaky voice]* Well, when I see the first star tonight, I'll wish I'm 6 feet tall and 300 pounds. I'll wish that I could eat you for dinner tonight!
	[Exit Lion *and* Mouse. *Enter* Wendy *and* Reindeer, *walking together]*
REINDEER:	The day is almost over now. Pretty soon the stars will begin to come out. Wendy, do you know what I'm going to wish on the first star?
WENDY:	What, Reindeer?
REINDEER:	Well, the only time people pay attention to me is at Christmastime. The rest of the year they don't even know I'm alive! So I'm going to wish that it will be Christmas all year long! And I'm going to wish that reindeer will be the most important and best-loved animals in the whole world!

WENDY:	That sounds like two wishes.
REINDEER:	So what? If I wish really hard, I just know I'll get what I want.
WENDY:	Well, I'm going to make a wish, too. I'm going to wish for a brand-new dress, just like the one my big sister has. And I know how to get my wish granted!
REINDEER:	You do?
WENDY:	Yes, but it's a secret.
REINDEER:	Oh, please tell me. I'm your friend, aren't I?
WENDY:	Well.... I suppose you're my friend, but....
REINDEER:	Friends are supposed to help each other, aren't they?
WENDY:	Well, OK.
REINDEER:	*[To audience]* I knew I'd get through to her!
WENDY:	Not very many people know this, so don't tell anyone else. *[Lowers voice]* If you climb to the top of the highest mountain, you'll be closer to the stars. If you are the very first one to wish on the evening star and you are standing at the top of the highest mountain, the evening star will grant your wish. She always does.
REINDEER:	Heh, heh! Thanks for telling me! *[Begins to hurry off]* I have to go now. Heh, heh, heh!
WENDY:	Where are you going?
REINDEER:	Oh, ah, I just remembered something I have to do.
WENDY:	Wait! I know what you're going to do! You're going to beat me to the top of the mountain, aren't you? That's not fair! I knew the secret first!
REINDEER:	Ha, ha. I can climb faster than you can! I have four long legs. You'll never catch up!
WENDY:	You've stolen my secret! Wait!

[Exit Reindeer. Star Bright approaches, wearing cape.]

STAR BRIGHT: Little girl, may I help you?

WENDY: Oh, who are you?

STAR BRIGHT: Star Bri-- I mean, Mrs. Bright, just old Mrs. Bright.

WENDY: I'm Wendy.

STAR BRIGHT: I heard you talking to that reindeer. I don't mean to be nosing into your business, but I know a shortcut to the mountain top. Come, I'll show you. I don't like that reindeer's attitude.

WENDY: But you're an old lady. How will you climb that mountain?

STAR BRIGHT: Oh, I will make my own way.

WENDY: OK. Show me!

[Wendy *and* Star Bright *begin walking.]*

WENDY: We'll have to hurry if we are going to beat that reindeer.

WENDY AND
STAR BRIGHT: *[Chanting together]*

We're going to wish upon a star—
Star light, star bright—
We're going to see the evening star,
And everything will be all right.

[Gray Cloud *enters and watches* Wendy *and* Star Bright. *Sinister music plays briefly.* Wendy *and* Star Bright *do not see* Gray Cloud.]

STAR BRIGHT: Wendy, do all people on earth wish only for things for themselves?

WENDY: I never thought about it.

[Sinister music, briefly]

WENDY: Was that a raindrop?

STAR BRIGHT: Rain? *[Looks behind her]* Oh, no! Gray Cloud!

WENDY: It's just a little rain.

STAR BRIGHT: You don't understand. I can't let that cloud catch up with me! Hurry, Wendy!

[Wendy *hurries on ahead and exits.* Gray Cloud *chases* Star Bright *as music plays.* Gray Cloud *finally chases* Star Bright *to stage left and covers her with a quilt, which puppeteer supplies from behind the stage.*]

STAR BRIGHT: *[Muffled]* Help! Help!

GRAY CLOUD: Heh, heh, heh! You'll never shine again! I'm going to leave you here. It will be dark soon. No one will find you. What fun for me! Your light has finally been put out!

[Gray Cloud *hovers at stage right as* Wendy *returns.*]

WENDY: Mrs. Bright, we have to hurry. I want to reach the mountain top before.... Where are you?

STAR BRIGHT: *[Muffled]* Help! Help!

WENDY: Mrs. Bright? Is that you? Are you under there? What has happened? *[Tugs at quilt]* This quilt is heavy! I can't lift it!

STAR BRIGHT: Get me out from under here!

WENDY: How did this happen? Who did this to you? This no ordinary quilt!

GRAY CLOUD: Heh, heh! She'll never be able to lift it on her own power! Ha, ha, ha!

[Curtain, *as sinister music plays*]

SCENE 3: Night, with Big Star in sky and tree in foreground

[On stage: Star Bright *beneath quilt—her cape has been removed; enter* Wendy.]

WENDY: I couldn't find anyone to help me. Oh, there's the first star of the evening. I don't see Reindeer at the top of the mountain. He didn't know about the shortcut. Maybe I am the first one to see the evening star tonight. Oh ... I wish ... I wish.... *[Looks down at dress, then at quilt]* I wish *[Slowly]* I could rescue Mrs. Bright from this heavy quilt.

[Wendy *gives the quilt a few more tugs and pulls it off* Star Bright, *who is no longer disguised with the cape.*]

WENDY: Mrs. Bright, what happened to you? You're not an old lady at all! You're a....

STAR BRIGHT: I'm Star Bright, the evening star. I got tired of granting the wishes of selfish people. I came to earth to see if I could find one truly unselfish person. Wendy, I found you. You used your wish to save me.

WENDY: I guess I didn't really need a new dress after all.

STAR BRIGHT: Thank you, Wendy. I have to go back to the sky now. I've learned that some people may use their wishes to help others. That thought will keep me happy as I shine in the sky from now on.

WENDY: Good-bye, Mrs. Bri-- I mean, Star Bright.

STAR BRIGHT: Good-bye, Wendy. Look for me tomorrow night.

[Curtain]

SCENE 4: Night sky with small stars and Star Bright

[On stage: Narrator]

NARRATOR: So Star Bright shines in the sky every night, granting the wish of the first person to see her each evening.

[Puppets enter as their names are spoken and exit when Narrator *finishes telling about them.]*

NARRATOR: Oh—you were wondering about the lion? He's still trying to catch that mouse. And the mouse? He's still only 3 inches tall. And the reindeer? He's still only around in December. The rest of the time he's at the North Pole.

REINDEER: Brr—it's cold up there! *[Exit]*

NARRATOR: And Wendy? When she wishes on the evening star, she sends a special greeting to Star Bright.

WENDY: Hi, friend!

NARRATOR: Oh, and Gray Cloud? He still manages to cover up most of the stars on a dark, cloudy night, but he can never cover Star Bright's light! Good night, everybody!

[Curtain, as closing music plays]

The Town Mouse and the Country Mouse

PUPPET-MAKING NOTES:
Complete patterns for all puppets are provided in chapter 2, figures 2.2 and 2.11-2.15.

CHARACTERS:
Narrator
Arthur, the mail carrier (Arthur was a rabbit
  in our production. See figure 2.2)
Henry, the country mouse
Lucinda, the town mouse
Mrs. Brown, the town home owner
Kitty

SCENERY: See "Specific Scenery Suggestions" in
  chapter 4, especially figures 4.16-4.19.
Country home exterior (house, mailbox, hill)
Country home interior (kitchen)

Town home exterior
Town home interior (dining room with food
  on table)

MUSIC:
Country music (peaceful)
Chase music

PROPS:
Suitcase for Lucinda
Mail pouch for Arthur

ꞁꞁꞁ

SCENE 1:	Country home exterior
	[Onstage: Narrator *and* Henry; *peaceful music plays briefly.]*
NARRATOR:	Once upon a time, there was a mouse who lived in the country. His name was Henry L. Mouse. His neighbors and friends called him Henry. He lived in a small, tidy cottage at the base of a hill. One bright summer day, Henry received a letter in the mail.
	[Exit Narrator; *enter* Arthur*]*
ARTHUR:	Howdy, Henry.
HENRY:	Good afternoon, Arthur.
ARTHUR:	Got some mail for you. Let's see ... here it is.
HENRY:	Thank you, Arthur. Hmm ... a cheese bill, an advertisement, an envelope of coupons for corn and grain. Oh, here's a letter from my cousin Lucinda.

ARTHUR: Lucinda? She lives over the hill, in the city, doesn't she?

HENRY: Yes. She lives in a large townhouse on Spenser Boulevard. She's lived there all her life.

ARTHUR: Spenser Boulevard, hmm? That's a mighty fine part of town.

HENRY: Oh! She writes that she's coming here for a visit this weekend. I haven't seen her for five years.

ARTHUR: Well, then, it will be nice to see her, won't it?

HENRY: Yes, Arthur, I suspect it will.

ARTHUR: More mail to deliver, so I must be on my way. Good day, Henry!

HENRY: Good-bye, Arthur.

[*Exit* Arthur *and* Henry, *while peaceful music plays*]

[*Curtain*]

SCENE 2: Country home interior

[*Onstage:* Narrator *and* Henry]

NARRATOR: Lucinda arrived on Friday evening with two large suitcases. Henry couldn't imagine why his cousin would need so many clothes for one weekend, but he was too polite to ask. Lucinda put away her belongings in the guest room and freshened up. Then she joined Henry in his cozy kitchen.

[*Enter* Lucinda]

NARRATOR: The cousins had much to talk about. They spent the evening catching up on each other's lives and activities.

[*Exit* Narrator]

LUCINDA: But what else do you do besides visit your neighbors and read the newspaper out on your front porch?

HENRY: Well, sometimes I go for a stroll through a cornfield.

LUCINDA: A cornfield?

HENRY: The sweetest corn grows in this part of the country. I often bring some back for supper.

LUCINDA: So you walk through cornfields. But what else is there to do around here?

HENRY: Well, if I want a little more exercise, I swim in the creek. It's a little muddy, but it feels nice on warm days.

LUCINDA: *[Sarcastically]* How exciting! But I don't think I'll swim while I'm here this weekend. Aren't there any interesting places to go around here—theaters, department stores, parties? Oh, I do love a good party!

HENRY: There's Mr. Jones's General Store. I can usually pick up some nice cracker crumbs from the floor. And if I'm lucky, there's a sprinkling of flour or oats on the counter.

LUCINDA: Crumbs? Oats? But what about cakes and pies, Chinese tea leaves, blueberry tarts? What you need is some refinement, some culture that can only be found in town.

HENRY: But I'm happy with cracker crumbs and oats and visiting my neighbors. They suit me.

LUCINDA: Nonsense! Come with me to the city. Let me show you how I live. Please come back with me tomorrow.

HENRY: Tomorrow? But I thought you were going to stay here until Sunday.

LUCINDA: *[To audience]* I'd die of boredom by then!

HENRY: What, Cousin Lucinda?

LUCINDA: Oh, just a change in plans. I really must go back tomorrow morning. But you may come with me. In fact, I insist!

HENRY: All right, but let's have supper now.

LUCINDA: Field corn and oats?

HENRY: Why, yes.

LUCINDA: I was afraid of that. Let me treat you, Henry, to a splendid feast.

HENRY: But we're not going to town until tomorrow.

LUCINDA:	I brought it with me! *[Exits and returns with suitcase]* Look—bakery bread, creamed corn, and look at these fancy currant buns with such tiny seeds on top!
HENRY:	You brought all this in your suitcase?
LUCINDA:	Yes, Henry, so I could show you how I live. You need a taste of the fine life, cousin!

[Enter Narrator]

NARRATOR:	So Henry and Lucinda ate bakery bread, creamed corn, and currant buns. Henry had a little trouble with the corn, as it kept slipping off his paws.
LUCINDA:	That's OK, Henry. You simply are not used to such delicacies. You'll learn, in time, to eat like a king!

[Curtain]

SCENE 3:	Town home exterior

[Enter Lucinda and Henry]

LUCINDA:	Ah, home at last!
HENRY:	It's quite a large house. In which part do you live?
LUCINDA:	I live on the first floor, near the dining room. But, of course, I roam all over the house, mostly at night, when the people are asleep and the cat is out.
HENRY:	Cat???
LUCINDA:	Didn't I mention her?
HENRY:	No, you never said anything about a cat. You live in the very same house with a c-c-cat?
LUCINDA:	One gets used to it. I just have to be careful.
HENRY:	A cat! I knew I should have stayed home! I could be sitting on the porch with the newspaper now, in perfect safety!
LUCINDA:	Let's go in.

HENRY:	Well, OK, but let's hurry and get to your room. *[Starts forward]*
LUCINDA:	Wait! *[Pulls Henry back]*
HENRY:	*[Whispering]* What's wrong?
LUCINDA:	It's Mrs. Brown, who owns the house.
	[Enter Mrs. Brown]
MRS. BROWN:	Kitty! Kitty! Where are you? Oh, Kitty, you were out all night and all morning. Where can you be?
	[Mrs. Brown searches around. Mice huddle to one side.]
MRS. BROWN:	Kitty, I have a nice bowl of milk for you.
	[Enter Kitty]
KITTY:	Meow, here I am.
MRS. BROWN:	I knew that would bring you back. Come on in, Kitty.
KITTY:	Wait a minute. Do I smell mice?
	[Mice shiver]
MRS. BROWN:	Come in, Kitty, Kitty.
KITTY:	Oh, well. There will be time for mice later. Ah, warm milk! Meow.
	[Exit Mrs. Brown and Kitty]
LUCINDA:	It's safe now. Kitty will be busy with her milk for a while.
HENRY:	If I had known about all this, I never would have come here. Let's hurry.
	[Exit Lucinda and Henry]
	[Curtain]

SCENE 4: Town home interior

[Onstage: Narrator*]*

NARRATOR: Henry spent a miserable day huddling in a corner of Lucinda's room. Finally, that evening, he had to admit that he was hungry and tired of staying in one corner. He was also a bit curious about the house in which his cousin lived. It certainly was grand, huge, and luxurious.

[Exit Narrator; *enter* Lucinda *and* Henry*]*

LUCINDA: Wait until you see the dining room, Henry!

HENRY: It looks like the Browns have just finished dinner. What a feast! Ham, muffins, and fresh green beans.

LUCINDA: And chocolate cake! The Browns feast like this nearly every night. And guess who else does.

HENRY: You?

LUCINDA: Me!

HENRY: But the cat! And the people!

LUCINDA: I just have to be careful. Come on! Let's eat!

[Enter Mrs. Brown; *mice huddle to one side.]*

MRS. BROWN: I'll just clear away some of these dishes now. Let's see ... I'd better cover up that cake so it doesn't dry out. There. Now where's that Kitty? She'll like some leftover ham.

[Exit Mrs. Brown*]*

LUCINDA: OK. Now we'll eat. She'll be busy with the cat and the dishes for a while.

HENRY: These muffins are good!

LUCINDA: Taste the beans!

HENRY: Oh, these are wonderful!

[Enter Mrs. Brown*]*

LUCINDA:	Didn't I tell you how fabulous it is here? I wouldn't give up this life for anything!
HENRY:	I have to admit, this is delicious. But the food is so rich! You eat like this every day?
LUCINDA:	You get used to it quickly.
MRS. BROWN:	Eeek! Mice!
HENRY:	Oh, no!
MRS. BROWN:	Get out of here, you creatures!
LUCINDA:	Quick, Henry, run to the doorway!
MRS. BROWN:	Kitty, Kitty, get in here! It's your job to keep mice away!! Kitty!
	[Enter Kitty*]*
KITTY:	Meow, meow! Oh boy, mice! Tasty morsels for dessert after that milk and ham!
	*[*Kitty *chases* Henry*]*
LUCINDA:	Run, Henry!
KITTY:	Here, mousie, mousie, mousie!
LUCINDA:	Run!
HENRY:	Help!
	[Chase music, as Kitty *chases the mice around the stage. Mice scream for help;* Mrs. Brown *yells "Eek!" Finally,* Kitty *catches* Henry *and holds him between her paws. Music ends.]*
KITTY:	I've got you now!
HENRY:	H-h-h-help!
KITTY:	The only question is, which part do I eat first? The head? The tail? Perhaps a little leg. Oh, what fun!

[Lucinda sneaks up behind Kitty and pulls her tail. Kitty turns quickly and drops Henry]

KITTY: Ouch! Who's that?

LUCINDA: Let's go!

HENRY: I'm going home!

[Exit mice]

KITTY: Ah, well, next time!

[Curtain]

SCENE 5: Country home exterior

[On stage: Narrator and Henry; peaceful music]

NARRATOR: So Henry returned to his cottage in the country. Lucinda got over her scare with the cat and stayed to feast on ham and muffins. She never really understood why Henry preferred the country life. She favored, instead, the excitement and the luxury of the town. She wrote to her cousin from time to time, and her letters were always full of the wonderful things she had seen and done.

[Exit Narrator; enter Arthur]

ARTHUR: Howdy, Henry.

HENRY: Good morning, Arthur.

ARTHUR: You ever going back to town?

HENRY: No, Arthur, I'm home for good.

ARTHUR: Why is that?

HENRY: Oh, just a slight difference of opinion between my cousin and myself.

ARTHUR: Well, as long as Lucinda has what she wants and you have what you want, I don't see any problem.

HENRY: No, Arthur, I don't see any problem either. Good day!

[Final curtain]

Percy's Tale, or Behind the Doors

PUPPET-MAKING NOTES:
Complete patterns for all characters are provided in chapter 2, figures 2.19-2.24.

CHARACTERS:
Percy, the bookworm
Taran Tarantula
Wolfgang Wolf
Flame the Dragon
Cinnamon Bear
Magic the Owl

SCENERY: Six doors (door-shaped cardboard attached to thin dowel rods). The dowel rods are mounted on a 1-by-2-inch board of wood, with holes drilled through the board for the rods, allowing the doors to be "opened" by turning the rods at the bottom, out of sight of the audience. Figure 4.15, in chapter 4, will make this clear. The doors are located near the background curtain behind the area where the puppets perform. During scenes 1 through 3, the doors are hidden by a black curtain, which is the only other scenery needed. At the beginning of scene 4, the curtain is flipped back to reveal the doors.

For variety, the fronts of the doors could resemble doors of different types, such as an ordinary household front door, a castle drawbridge, a barn door, etc.

The back of each door shows the following:

- a cliff with a steep drop-off

- a picture to represent the book *Julie of the Wolves* by Jean Craighead George (picture should include title and author)

- a picture to represent *Charlotte's Web* by E. B. White (the spider must be prominent)

- a picture to represent *Anansi the Spider* by Gerald McDermott

- a picture of a menacing, fire-breathing dragon

- a picture to represent *Paddington's Lucky Day* (or another Paddington book by Michael Bond)

OTHER MATERIALS AND REFERENCE LIST:
A piece of paper, rolled up and tied with a ribbon (small enough for Wolfgang to hold)

Copies of the following books, if available, for display after the puppet show (or other books by the same authors and other books featuring friendly dragons)

Bond, Michael, and Fred Banbery. *Paddington's Lucky Day.* New York: Random House, 1974.

Cosgrove, Stephen. *The Muffin Muncher.* Mankato, Minn.: Creative Education, 1979.

George, Jean Craighead. *Julie of the Wolves.* New York: Harper & Row, 1972.

Grahame, Kenneth. *The Reluctant Dragon.* Philadelphia: Dufour Editions, 1959.

Hildick, E. W. *The Dragon That Lived Under Manhattan.* New York: Crown, 1970.

McDermott, Gerald. *Anansi the Spider.* New York: Holt, Rinehart & Winston, 1972.

Muller, Romeo. *Puff the Magic Dragon.* New York: Avon/Camelot, 1979.

Pomerantz, Charlotte. *Detective Poufy's First Case.* Reading, Mass.: Addison-Wesley, 1976.

Tillstrom, Burr. *The Dragon Who Lived Downstairs.* New York: Morrow, 1984.

Timm, Stephen. *The Dragon and the Mouse.* Fargo, N. Dak.: Timm, 1980.

White, E. B. *Charlotte's Web.* New York: Harper, 1952.

SCENE 1: *[Enter* Percy, *carrying book. Walks to center stage, reading silently.]*

PERCY: *[Looking up]* Oh, hello! Where did you come from? I guess I wasn't paying attention to where I was going. *[Pause]* Who am I? Oh, I'm Percy. I'm a bookworm, in case you hadn't noticed. I like to read stories, but, oh, I like to tell stories, too! Do you mind if I tell you what happened just the other day? Good. Let's see … it all began with Wolfgang Wolf and Taran Tarantula….

[Enter Wolfgang *and* Taran, *running and gasping for breath]*

TARAN: Is he chasing us?

WOLFGANG: I don't know. I think so, but I just can't go on. We have to rest.

PERCY: Wolfgang, Taran, what's wrong?

TARAN: We can't stop to explain! We've got to get away and hide!

WOLFGANG: But I can't take one more step! Oh, what will we do?

PERCY: Come on into my tunnel. It's small, but you'll be safe for a while.

[All characters move to stage left.]

PERCY: Now, tell me what's wrong. Why were you running?

TARAN: Oh, it's terrible!

WOLFGANG: Percy, we've just escaped from the cave of Flame the Dragon.

PERCY: Flame? You mean that huge, green, fire-breathing monster?

WOLFGANG: Yes, yes, that's the one! He caught us and our friend Cinnamon Bear, and he's been holding us captive for three days! Taran and I managed to escape when he was cooking his dinner last night.

TARAN: You see, the fire he breathes is so hot that he has to go outside to cook, so he doesn't burn up his cave.

WOLFGANG: We waited for just the right moment, and because it was already dark, Flame couldn't see us as we slipped out and went behind the cave. We started to run, but Cinnamon wasn't with us!

TARAN:	Flame must have come back before Cinnamon could escape.
WOLFGANG:	We wanted to go back for him, but we knew Flame would capture us again if we did.
TARAN:	Flame kept threatening to cook us for dinner if we tried to get away.
WOLFGANG:	So we ran and ran all night.
TARAN:	And now we must find someone powerful enough to help us defeat Flame and rescue Cinnamon Bear.
PERCY:	Maybe I can do something.
TARAN:	You? You're so little!
WOLFGANG:	Bookworms can't fight dragons!
PERCY:	I'm not talking about fighting. I have a friend who may be able to help.
TARAN:	I think we should just keep running and get as far away from Flame as we can.
WOLFGANG:	But what about Cinnamon?
PERCY:	That's right! You can't just leave him in Flame's cave. *[Pause]* Now listen to me. Go over the bridge and across the meadow, until you come to the hollow oak tree. Magic the Owl lives there. She is my friend. She may have an idea of how to rescue Cinnamon.
TARAN:	*[Slowly]* Well ... it's our only hope right now. Let's go.
WOLFGANG:	Thank you, Percy. Let's hurry, Taran. I shudder to think what Flame is planning to cook for breakfast today!

[All exit]

[Curtain]

SCENE 2:   *[Onstage:* Flame *and* Cinnamon Bear*]*

FLAME: Heh, heh, heh! You're still my prisoner!

CINNAMON: *[Trying to be brave]* Well, just wait till my friends come back with help!

FLAME: They'll never come back for you. They're so afraid of me, I'll bet they haven't stopped running yet!

                 (Sings)   The fire I breathe
                                    Is so red hot,
                                    You'll find out how much
                                    Steam I've got!
                                    I'll throw some
                                    Spiders in the pot,
                                    Some tongue of wolf
                                    And then an eel,
                                    A moldy, rotten
                                    Apple peel,   *[Moves close to* Cinnamon*]*
                                    Then YOU — You'll be
                                    My very next meal!

                 *[*Cinnamon *backs away]*

CINNAMON: But why?

FLAME: I told you yesterday. I don't like bears! What good are you? Oh, little children like stuffed teddy bears, but most people just don't like you. Bears get into people's food when they go camping. Bears scare people. Why, I'd be doing the world a favor if I captured each and every one of you and made bear stew of you all!

CINNAMON: But — but what about Wolfgang and Taran? They....

FLAME: Oh, they're even worse! Why, look at all the stories that have been written. Wolves are always bad, bad, bad. Who was the bad guy in "The Three Little Pigs"? A wolf! Who was the villain in "Little Red Riding Hood"? A wolf! And spiders are just the same! Who frightened away Little Miss Muffet? A spider! A big, ugly furry spider like your friend. I told them yesterday, I'd like to see them show me one wolf, one spider, one bear who is not a villain, a bad guy, a despicable creature! Just one! I'll bet they can't do it!

CINNAMON: What if they do? What if they can prove to you that all of us are not bad or frightening?

FLAME: I told them yesterday, if they can do that, I'll let you go. But don't count on it. They'll never succeed.

[Curtain]

SCENE 3: *[Onstage:* Wolfgang, Taran *and* Magic*]*

WOLFGANG: So you see, Magic, that's the problem! Do you know of any way to prove to Flame that some of us are nice, or friendly, or helpful?

TARAN: Or should we just give up and get someone powerful to help us fight the dragon?

MAGIC: No, don't give up. Hmm ... let me think. Yes ... there's a trail you can follow and some doors you may open along the way. Those doors will reveal the answers you seek. But it's a trail of dangers as well as answers. I will start you on your way, but you must make some decisions as you go along.

TARAN: What do you mean?

MAGIC: Behind some doors lie the clues to solve your problem. But if you choose the wrong doors, you will be in danger again. It's up to you. My magical powers will not do it all. You must choose. Percy will meet you at the end of the trail. My thoughts will be with you. Good-bye, and good luck.

[Curtain]

SCENE 4: Black curtain is flipped back to reveal the doors.

[Onstage: Wolfgang *and* Taran*]*

WOLFGANG: There it is!

TARAN: The trail of doors!

WOLFGANG: And behind each door, the answer....

TARAN: Or danger!

WOLFGANG: Let's go!

[Wolfgang and Taran approach the first two doors.]

TARAN: Which one do we choose?

WOLFGANG: I don't know. I think we just have to make a guess. Magic did not give us a clue; she said we have to decide.

TARAN: You go first.

WOLFGANG: OK.

[Wolfgang pushes open the first door to reveal a cliff.]

TARAN: *[Running toward door]* I don't see any....

WOLFGANG: No, Taran! Look! It's the edge of a cliff! *[Pulls Taran back]* Be careful!

[Wolfgang closes the door.]

WOLFGANG: That was close. But we had better try the next door.

TARAN: I'm afraid.

WOLFGANG: We have to try. Think about poor Cinnamon Bear.

TARAN: OK. I guess it's my turn.

[Taran slowly pushes open the second door to reveal Julie of the Wolves.*]*

TARAN: I don't get it.

WOLFGANG: Me either. *[Pause]* Wait a minute. *Julie of the Wolves* by Jean Craighead George. That's the title of a book.

TARAN: So?

WOLFGANG: I've read it. *Julie of the Wolves. [Pause]* Oh my goodness. Taran, I think I understand now! This is the story of an Eskimo girl who gets lost in Alaska.

TARAN: I still don't understand.

WOLFGANG: The wolves befriend her! They help her! Taran, don't you see? Here is proof. Here's the proof we need to show Flame that all wolves are not bad. In this story, the wolves are good! Let's keep going!

[Taran and Wolfgang move to the next pair of doors.]

TARAN: Which one? Which one? What's behind those doors?

WOLFGANG: Let's find out.

[Wolfgang pushes open the third door to reveal Charlotte's Web.]

WOLFGANG: *Charlotte's Web* by E. B. White.

TARAN: I know that story! My grandmother read it with me! Charlotte is a spider, a kind and loving spider. Why, she saved the life of her friend. Wait till Flame hears about this!

WOLFGANG: Let's go on. There are more doors.

[Wolfgang pushes open the fourth door to reveal Anansi the Spider.]

TARAN: *Anansi the Spider* by Gerald McDermott.... Anansi. I don't know who that is.

WOLFGANG: You should! Anansi is a spider in African folktales. In one of the tales, Anansi is responsible for placing the moon in the sky.

TARAN: Wait till Flame hears about this! Two different spiders who do good things. Oh, boy, let's go!

[Taran and Wolfgang move to the last two doors. Taran quickly pushes open the fifth door to reveal the dragon.]

TARAN AND WOLFGANG: Aaahh! *[Slam door]*

TARAN: Was that Blaze?

WOLFGANG: Yes. Blaze is Flame's cousin. Flame must have sent Blaze to find us.

TARAN: Hurry! Let's move on!

WOLFGANG: Be careful! Don't open the door all the way!

TARAN: OK. Here we go.

[Taran opens sixth door slowly.]

TARAN: *Paddington's Lucky Day* by Michael Bond.

WOLFGANG: Paddington is a bear that people love, not just little children, but older ones, too. School-age children read about Paddington. And even their parents love him.

TARAN: He's the bear that lives with a family in England, isn't he?

WOLFGANG: Yes, and even when things go wrong and he causes problems, he never does it on purpose, and he's always forgiven.

TARAN: That's it, Wolfgang! We've done it!

WOLFGANG: One wolf, one bear....

TARAN: And two spiders!

WOLFGANG: All the proof we need is right here in these books.

[Enter Percy. Wolfgang and Taran rush to side of stage, away from Percy.]

PERCY: *[Calling]* Wolfgang and Taran, did Magic help you?

WOLFGANG: *[Turning toward Percy]* Yes, she did.

TARAN: *[To Wolfgang]* Come on, come on, let's go.

PERCY: Where are you going in such a hurry?

TARAN: To get copies of those books. We have to show them to Flame. And we have to hurry to save Cinnamon Bear.

[Percy moves toward Taran and Wolfgang.]

PERCY: Wait! Give this to Flame, too. *[Hands Wolfgang a piece of paper]*

WOLFGANG: OK. Let's go!

[Curtain]

SCENE 5:	*[Onstage:* Magic. *Enter* Wolfgang, Taran *and* Cinnamon.*]*
WOLFGANG:	We came to thank you, Magic, for pointing the way.
TARAN:	But we have to ask you, did we succeed in traveling that trail because of your magical powers?
MAGIC:	No, Taran. You and Wolfgang made it safely through the doors yourselves. You recognized the clues. I didn't need to use my powers because I knew you could do it! And I knew Flame would change his mind about you and let Cinnamon go when he saw those books for himself.
WOLFGANG:	But what really changed Flame's mind was the sheet of paper Percy had us take to the dragon.
MAGIC:	Oh? What was on that piece of paper?
TARAN:	A long list of books! *The Muffin Muncher, The Reluctant Dragon, Puff the Magic Dragon, The Dragon Who Lived Downstairs.*
CINNAMON:	Those are just four of the titles.
WOLFGANG:	And in every one of those stories, there is a dragon—a nice dragon who doesn't terrorize others by breathing fire and taking captives.
CINNAMON:	With all those stories, I think we convinced him that dragons don't have to be villains.
MAGIC:	Where is Flame now?
TARAN:	Oh, he's back in his cave.
WOLFGANG:	I think he'll be there for a long time. He's settled down with a huge stack of books to read!
ALL:	*[To audience]* Won't you read, too?
	[Curtain]

The Cat and Mouse in Partnership
Based on a fairy tale by the Brothers Grimm

PUPPET-MAKING NOTES:

For the mouse pattern, use figure 2.13, and for the cat, figure 2.15, in chapter 2. A bow tie may be attached with hook and loop fasteners each time the cat goes out.

CHARACTERS:
    Cat
    Mouse

SCENERY: One divided background:
- interior of house at stage left
- interior of church at stage right

PROP: Pot of fat (may be two-dimensional cardboard pot on a stick held by a puppeteer so the puppets will appear to carry it)

⸎⸎⸎

SCENE 1:   *[Onstage:* Cat *and* Mouse *in front of house interior, stage left]*

CAT: Little mouse, as we are such good friends and have known each other for quite some time, let me make an unusual suggestion.

MOUSE: What is that, Cat?

CAT: I propose that you and I set up housekeeping together.

MOUSE: Live together? A cat and a mouse? You are right—that is a very unusual suggestion!

CAT: I know that under other circumstances, it probably would not work, but you and I are friends. We trust each other, don't we?

MOUSE: We ... yes, yes, we do.

CAT: So do you agree? Shall we share a home and keep house here together?

MOUSE: There is something to be said for sharing chores and belongings. Yes, I agree; it makes sense.

CAT: Good! Now then, we must think about storing up some food for the winter, or we will starve when the snow covers the ground.

MOUSE: Yes, we do not want to go hungry. Remember the pot of fat I bought last week? It will keep nicely until we need it. I will get it. *[Exits and returns with pot of fat.]*

CAT: Ah, yes. Tasty and filling. Quite a treat!

MOUSE: We must store it in a safe place where no one else will find it.

CAT: What about the cupboard?

MOUSE: No, I really think it should be kept farther away, out of our reach. We would not want to be tempted to get into it before we really need it.

CAT: Quite right, my dear. Well, let us think. My, it looks good! *[Sniffs pot]* And, oh, how heavenly it smells!

MOUSE: That's it!

CAT: What?

MOUSE: Heavenly! Let's store it in the church, under the altar. There could not be a better hiding place, for who would steal from a church?

CAT: Very well. I will take it there myself. You, little mouse, must not venture outside, for it is not safe. You might be caught in a trap or eaten by a cat who lacks the manners I have. I won't be long.

MOUSE: Hide it well!

CAT: Oh, I will.

[Cat picks up pot of fat, crosses to stage right, and places pot down.]

CAT: There we go, Safely hidden.

[Curtain]

SCENE 2: *[Onstage:* Cat, *stage left]*

CAT: *[To audience]* It has been two weeks since I hid the pot of fat in the church. I have thought about that delicious fat every day. I cannot stand it any longer. I must taste it. Just a little taste, and I will be satisfied. *[Pause]* But what excuse will I give for going out? And what if someone sees me going into the church? Hmmm.... *[Paces]* I know! That's it! *[Calling]* Mousie!

[Enter Mouse*]*

MOUSE: Yes, my friend?

CAT: I have been asked by my cousin to be godfather to her little son. The christening is today. He is furry with little brown and white patches, and I simply must be there.

MOUSE: Yes, certainly you should go. I will stay home and keep house. But while you are at the christening party, feasting and having fun, think of me, here at home, and do not be away too long.

CAT: Of course, my dear. Good-bye for now.

[Exit Mouse. Cat *moves stage right, goes to the pot, looks left and right, takes pot between his paws, and noisily licks the fat off the top.]*

CAT: Oh, this is wonderful. I'll just have a little. There ... just a little off the top. She'll never know the difference.

[Cat wipes whiskers and mouth and stretches.*]*

CAT: And now for a little nap. *[Lies down]*

[Enter Mouse *at stage left]*

MOUSE: I wonder why Cat has been gone so long.

[Cat gets up, stretches and yawns, and moves stage left, to *Mouse.]*

CAT: Here I am, home again!

MOUSE: I expect you had a nice time?

CAT: Nicer than you can imagine.

MOUSE: By the way, what name did the child receive?

CAT: Name? Oh, um ... Top-Off.

MOUSE: Top-Off? That's an unusual name, but a very fine one. Is it a common name in your family?

CAT: Common? No, not at all. In fact, this is the first one.

MOUSE: Come now. I have our supper ready.

CAT: Supper?

MOUSE: Oh, I suppose you're not hungry after the christening feast.

CAT: Hungry? No, not hungry at all.

      [Curtain]

SCENE 3:   *[Onstage:* Cat, *stage left]*

CAT: *[To audience]* I can't stand it! It's been four weeks since I tasted the fat in our little pot. I simply must have another taste! *[Looking left]* Mouse, dear!

MOUSE: *[Entering from left]* Did you call me?

CAT: Yes. I have another cousin who has had a baby. I have been asked to be godfather to this child, and I cannot refuse.

MOUSE: Very well. I will wait for you here. Say hello to your cousin for me.

CAT: I will. *[Crosses to stage right, and goes to pot of fat. Looks around, and then eats noisily.]*

CAT: Ah, nothing tastes quite as good as food I can keep all to myself! Oh, lovely, delicious secret! *[Stretches and yawns]* Just a short nap this time. *[Lies down]*

      [Enter Mouse, *stage left.* Cat *gets up and crosses to* Mouse.*]*

MOUSE: Hello! Was it a lovely christening?

CAT: Heavenly!

MOUSE: What name did they give this child?

CAT: Half-Gone.

MOUSE: Half-Gone! I have never in my entire life heard of such a name.

CAT: I think I will just go to bed now. It is not my fault that my cousin has chosen such a name. *[Exits]*

MOUSE: *[Shaking her head]* Half-Gone! Really! *[Pause]* Did he say "heavenly"?

      [Curtain]

SCENE 4:   *[Onstage:* Cat *and* Mouse, *stage left]*

CAT: Mouse, dear, once again I have been asked to be godfather to my cousin's child.

MOUSE: But, Cat, you just had a new nephew two weeks ago.

CAT: As good things come in three, I cannot refuse to go.

MOUSE: Top-Off, Half-Gone.... I cannot help but wonder what this one will be named. It is very curious indeed.

CAT: Well, you never go out into the world. You do not know about such matters. I will be home soon.

[Mouse exits, stage left. Cat *crosses right. He goes directly to the pot of fat and eats noisily.]*

CAT: Ah! So good! Now the pot is empty, and I don't have to be always thinking about the fat waiting here for me.

[Cat crosses to left. Enter Mouse.*]*

MOUSE: My, that was a quick trip.

CAT: Yes, yes, it was.

MOUSE: I suppose with all the practice you've had, you have this godfather business well in hand.

CAT: I don't think I'll be asked to be godfather again.

MOUSE: No? Well, what is the name of this child?

CAT: You'll find this name just as strange as the others. It is All-Gone.

MOUSE: All-Gone? Strange, indeed!

CAT: Do not ask me any more questions about this, for I am tired. *[Exit]*

MOUSE: All-Gone, indeed!

[Curtain]

SCENE 5:   *[Onstage:* Cat *and* Mouse, *stage left]*

MOUSE: Cat, winter is here. It has been three months since we safely stored away our little pot of fat. There is no more food to be found on the ground. We must go get our fat. How delicious it will taste here in our cozy home!

CAT: Of course the fat would taste good now.

MOUSE: Let us go together and fetch our winter food supply.

CAT: I suppose we must.

   *[*Cat *and* Mouse *cross right.* Mouse *picks up pot.]*

MOUSE: Empty! Empty! Now I understand what those names meant! I see what kind of partner you have been for me! You have not been called to be godfather three times. You have not been godfather at all! First Top-Off! Then Half-Gone! Then....

CAT: Be quiet, Mouse. One more word, and I will eat you, as well!

MOUSE: All-Gone!

   *[*Cat *leaps on* Mouse *and noisily eats her.* Mouse *puppet is pulled down behind stage by puppeteer.* Cat *wipes whiskers and mouth.]*

CAT: *[To audience]* That, my friends, is the way of the world. A mouse should never set up a partnership with a cat!

   [Curtain]

The Forest Princess

PUPPET-MAKING NOTES:
Complete patterns and directions for all puppets are provided in chapter 3.

CHARACTERS:
- Prince
- King
- Queen
- Felicia
- Leo, the lion cub
- Bear Cub
- Wolf
- Rottina
- Pamela

SCENERY: See "Specific Scenery Suggestions" in chapter 4.
- Throne room
- Forest
- Forest with waterfall

MUSIC:
- Felicia's music (soft, pretty music)
- Rottina's music (evil-sounding music)

٤٤٤

SCENE 1:   Throne room

[Onstage: Prince, King, Queen*]*

PRINCE: Mother, Father, you wished to see me?

KING: Yes, Son. Come here. We have a matter of great importance to discuss with you.

QUEEN: It concerns your future. As prince of this great kingdom, you need to think about that.

KING: You are old enough now to marry. Have you thought about that yet?

PRINCE: Yes, Father, I have thought about marriage. But I have not yet met the person who is right for me.

QUEEN: You should choose your future bride wisely, Son, for she will someday be queen of this land.

KING: Perhaps a princess from one of our neighboring countries.

QUEEN: Do you remember Princess Rottina, whom you met at the Halloween Ball last year? Her father has spoken to us and is quite willing to let her visit our kingdom and get to know you better.

KING: The fair and lovely Rottina is quite eager to visit.

PRINCE: Mother, Father, I remember Rottina very well. She was neither fair nor lovely. She cared only about how she looked, and she made fun of the other ladies at the ball.

QUEEN: That's no way to talk about a princess from one of our neighboring kingdoms.

PRINCE: I am NOT interested in the Princess Rottina. May I be excused now?

QUEEN: Yes, Son, but do think about this matter.

PRINCE: I will think about it, Mother, but I will not change my mind. *[Exit Prince]*

KING: Do not worry, my dear. Princess Rottina will be here for a visit soon. Perhaps she has changed. Her father so strongly wishes to make a match between her and our son.

QUEEN: It would be a good thing for our two kingdoms, wouldn't it?

KING: A good match for our kingdoms, yes.

  [Curtain]

SCENE 2: The forest

  [Enter Prince]

PRINCE: I am troubled by what my parents have said. I don't even know if I want to be married yet. And I know I do not want to marry Rottina. It is peaceful here in the forest. It is a good place to be alone and to think about my future. Someday I will be king of all this land!

  [Enter Felicia, Leo with bandage on paw, Wolf, and Bear Cub]

PRINCE: Who is this? I will hide near these trees and watch for a while.

  [Felicia's music, as she pets Leo]

FELICIA: Are you feeling better, Leo? I'm so glad I was able to free your paw from that trap.

LEO: It's getting better already, Felicia. Whatever you put on my paw is working wonders.

FELICIA: You'll be feeling like the Prince of the Forest again in a very short time. *[Turns to Bear Cub]* And you, my little cub, have you had enough to eat this morning?

BEAR CUB: Oh, yes, Felicia. Those berries were delicious. Thank you for showing me where to find the juciest ones.

FELICIA: You're quite welcome, my little one.

WOLF: Felicia, look, just beyond those trees. Someone is watching us.

LEO: Someone who does not come here often. Someone who may be a danger to the wild creatures of the forest.

BEAR CUB: Perhaps it isn't safe for us to stay here this morning.

FELICIA: You may be right. Let's go.

PRINCE: Wait! I only wish to meet you!

WOLF: Hurry, my friends.

              [Exit Felicia, Leo, Bear Cub, and Wolf]

PRINCE: How gentle she is with the animals. How kind she seems. But who is she? Who is this Felicia of the forest?

              [Curtain]

SCENE 3:   Throne room

              [Enter Rottina and Pamela, as Rottina's music plays]

ROTTINA: What a terrible journey! That coach driver was going slowly on purpose, just to anger me, the Princess Rottina.

PAMELA: The roads were rough and the rain made it difficult to see the way.

ROTTINA: Nonsense, Pamela! He did it on purpose! And the horses splashed mud all over my dress.

PAMELA: On purpose, I suppose.

ROTTINA: What?

PAMELA: Oh, nothing.

ROTTINA: Well, just remember that you are my lady-in-waiting. I'm the princess, and I am always right.

PAMELA: Yes, Princess Rottina.

ROTTINA: Well, where is the prince? He should have met me here. Some people have no manners!

PAMELA: I have heard that the prince is a kind man, and very good looking, too.

ROTTINA: If he were kind, he would not make me wait like this. *[Looks around]* Just look at the luxury of this palace! Velvet drapes! Golden goblets! I mean to marry the prince and be queen over all of this when he becomes king. He is a very rich man. And those riches can be mine!

[Enter Prince *and* King*]*

KING: Ah, Princess Rottina. So sorry to keep you waiting.

ROTTINA: Humph!

KING: Son, you remember the lovely Rottina from our neighboring kingdom.

PRINCE: Hello, Rottina.

KING: Doesn't she look nice today?

PRINCE: *[Pausing]* Uh, yes.

ROTTINA: *[Overly sweetly]* Why, thank you.

KING: I trust you had a good journey?

ROTTINA: No, it was terri-- ... I mean, oh, yes. The coach and driver you sent for me were just perfect.

PAMELA: She was just telling me what she thought of the journey in your coach.

KING: How long will you be staying with us, Princess Rottina?

ROTTINA: I will stay for about a week. *[To audience]* Or as long as it takes to win over the prince.

PRINCE: A week? That long?

KING: How lovely it will be to have you as our guest.

[Sound of dog barking]

ROTTINA: A dog! Well, keep it away from me! And see to it that his barking stops!

PRINCE: He is merely excited at having visitors. He wants to come in and greet you.

KING: No, Son. I don't think that will be wise.

ROTTINA: Lock it up in a cage while I am here! I will not have it jumping on me with its dirty paws!

PRINCE: I will not lock up my pet. Where I stay, he will stay.

KING: Perhaps we can keep him in another room.

PRINCE: I will go to him. His company will be more pleasant than the company in here. *[Exit]*

PAMELA: Winning over the prince may be harder than you thought — perhaps too big a job for you!

ROTTINA: Give me time, Pamela. What I want, I usually get.

KING: We will see you at dinner, Princess Rottina. Perhaps you would both like to freshen up now.

PAMELA: Thank you, Your Majesty.

ROTTINA: I expect that the best room has been reserved for me!

             [Exit Rottina and Pamela]

             [Curtain]

SCENE 4:   The forest

             [Onstage: Prince]

PRINCE: Only here in the forest is there peace and quiet. Rottina never stops complaining. Why can't my father see what she is really like?

             [Felicia's music, as Felicia and Wolf enter]

PRINCE: The lady of the forest! I will try to speak with her. Fair lady! No, don't run away this time. Please wait. I am the prince. I only wish to meet you.

WOLF: *[To* Felicia*]* It is the prince. I can see that now.

FELICIA: *[Bowing]* Your Majesty, it is an honor to meet you. I am Felicia.

PRINCE: Felicia, I have watched you with the forest animals. Why are they not afraid of you? And why do you have no fear of them? Has someone cast a magic spell over the wild creatures of the forest?

FELICIA: Only the spell of love and trust. The animals do not fear me because they know I will not hurt them. I have won their trust. They know I love them.

WOLF: Felicia is the kindest human we have ever met. None of us would ever hurt her. She has helped us, and in return we protect and love her.

PRINCE: Do you live in the forest, Felicia?

FELICIA: Yes. It is here that I am most comfortable, with the animals.

PRINCE: I would so much like to get to know you. Will you come and spend tomorrow afternoon at the palace? I would like you to meet my mother and father, the queen and the king.

FELICIA: I would be honored to be a guest at the palace.

PRINCE: I would be honored to have you as my guest. But for now, I would love to walk with you here in the forest and get to know you.

[Prince and Felicia *move to one side of the stage.]*

WOLF: *[To audience]* And so Felicia and the prince spent the afternoon walking and talking and learning about each other's lives—the royal life of the prince in his palace and the simple life Felicia led in the forest. Felicia taught the prince about the animals of the forest. And he began to notice things he had never seen before: the many shades of green in the leaves of the trees, tiny pink and purple wildflower buds, the tracks of animals in the soft earth, the golden glow of the sun beyond the trees. And the prince felt a happiness begin to grow inside him, and Felicia felt it, too.

[Curtain]

SCENE 5: Throne room

[Onstage: King *and* Queen; *enter* Prince *and* Felicia*]*

PRINCE: Mother, Father, I would like you to meet Felicia.

FELICIA: I am most honored to meet you, my king and queen.

KING: Then you are from our kingdom?

PRINCE: Felicia lives in the forest, Mother and Father. She has tamed the wild creatures there. They have no fear of her and pose no danger to her.

QUEEN: Son, may we speak with you alone for a moment?

FELICIA: I will go into the other room so you may speak freely. I thought I heard a dog in there. May I play with him?

PRINCE: Of course, Felicia. Right through this door.

            [Exit Felicia]

KING: This lady you have found in the forest is very pretty and seems quite kind, but....

PRINCE: But what, Father? What can be more important than kindness?

QUEEN: Son, we can see that you are in love with her already. But as prince of this kingdom, you may never marry her. She is only a poor country girl.

KING: You must make a proper match with a lady from a noble family, or a princess. For you will someday be king.

            [Rottina's music, as Rottina enters]

QUEEN: Why, hello, Rottina. I hope you enjoyed your lunch.

ROTTINA: It was acceptable. Who is that ragged person playing with your dog in the other room?

KING: Just one of the peasant women from the forest.

ROTTINA: Well, I was looking for you, my prince. Shall we go for a walk together? We have some talking to do.

PRINCE: Perhaps later, Rottina. I must go speak with someone right now and apologize for the way my parents are acting. *[Exit Prince]*

QUEEN: Don't worry, Rottina. Felicia is very beautiful, but she will be no threat to you.

KING: You must give the prince some more time. He will come to see which one of you will make the best queen.

ROTTINA: *[Calling]* Pamela! Come here!

             [Enter Pamela*]*

PAMELA: Yes, Rottina?

ROTTINA: We have some plans to make, Pamela. I need your help.

PAMELA: Plans? What plans are those?

ROTTINA: Why, wedding plans, of course. With the king and queen on my side, how can I lose?

PAMELA: *[To audience]* But she must have the prince on her side as well.

ROTTINA: Come on, come on. Let's get to work!

             [Exit Rottina *and* Pamela. *Enter* Prince *and* Felicia*]*

PRINCE: Mother and Father, I know you want me to think about marriage. I have thought about it, and perhaps I am ready to marry.

QUEEN: That's welcome news to us. You need a princess to help you prepare for the day that you become king.

PRINCE: But Princess Rottina is not the one I wish to marry.

KING: Now, see here, Son....

PRINCE: Rottina does not really care about me. She cares only about our palace, our riches, and her clothing. Felicia is the one I want to marry. And, just as important, she wants to marry me.

QUEEN: But we cannot allow it!

PRINCE: You don't even know Felicia! You have not given her a chance.

KING: All right, all right. I will agree to your marriage....

QUEEN: What?

KING: Wait. Felicia, I will agree to your marriage to our son if you can prove your worth, your cleverness, your courage.

FELICIA: How must I do that, sir?

PRINCE: Father, this is not right. Why should she have to prove herself, merely because she is not of noble birth? Rottina did not have to prove anything.

FELICIA: It is all right. I will do what he asks, for then perhaps he will come to know me and to accept me.

KING: I will consent to your marriage to my son if you can complete three tasks within the next three days.

FELICIA: I am listening.

KING: First, you must bring me a lock of hair from the mane of the great lion of the forest. Second, you must bring back a carpet woven of the pine needles which lie on the floor of the forest. Third, you must show me the silver hidden deep within the forest — silver enough for a lifetime. You have three days to complete these tasks — if indeed you can!

FELICIA: Very well, Your Majesty. I will return in three days' time.

PRINCE: I will walk with you to the forest, Felicia.

               [Exit Felicia *and* Prince*]*

QUEEN: What if she is able to complete the three tasks? Then we must allow her to marry our son.

KING: Have no fear, my queen. Felicia will never complete the tasks.

QUEEN: How do you know that?

KING: Even if she were somehow able to get a lock of the great lion's mane, and even if she were to stay up for three days and nights weaving a carpet of pine needles, Felicia will never complete the third task I have given her.

QUEEN: What makes you so sure of that?

KING: Because — heh, heh — there is no silver hidden in the forest! I made that part up!

QUEEN: That is horrible! That is dishonest! That is very, very clever of you, my dear! Come along now. We have some houseguests to entertain.

[Exit King *and* Queen*]*

[Curtain]

SCENE 6:   The forest

[Enter Prince *and* Felicia*]*

PRINCE: Only three days, Felicia. If you do not complete the tasks my father has given you, I will lose you forever!

FELICIA: I must try! I love you, and I mean to marry you. I will take one task at a time. *[Pause]* The first one is easy. Not long ago I did a favor for a lion cub caught in a trap. I freed him and bandaged his paw.

[Enter Leo*]*

FELICIA: He told me that if I ever needed anything from him, I should just ask. And here is that lion cub now.

LEO: Good day, Felicia. Oh, you are not alone.

FELICIA: This is the prince, Leo. He will not harm you.

LEO: Did I hear you say you needed me, Felicia?

FELICIA: Yes, Leo, I need your help. I need you to go to your father, the great lion of the forest, and bring back a lock from his mane.

LEO: A lock of my father's mane?

PRINCE: You see, Leo, my father, the king, has given Felicia three tasks to do within three days' time. This is the first of the three.

LEO: Have no worry, gentle lady. I will go to my father. He will not refuse any favor you ask.

FELICIA: Thank you, my little friend.

[Exit Leo*]*

PRINCE: I must return to the castle, Felicia. My parents are giving a special dinner tonight in honor of their guest.

FELICIA: Princess Rottina?

PRINCE: Princess! You act more like a princess than she does! I wish I did not have to attend the dinner, but my parents have given me no choice.

FELICIA: Farewell, my prince. These tasks I must do alone. I will see you in three days' time. Do not worry. We will be together soon.

PRINCE: Farewell, my princess. *[Exit Prince]*

FELICIA: Now for task number two. *[Looks around]* There are certainly plenty of pine needles. Now, to gather them up and use some threads from my skirt to weave them together.

              [Felicia's music, as she gathers pine needles]

FELICIA: It's no use. At this rate, it will take weeks to weave a carpet from these pine needles. It's hopeless! I'll never marry my prince! *[Cries herself to sleep]*

              [Enter Wolf and Bear Cub]

WOLF: Oh, it is Felicia!

BEAR CUB: She is asleep. She looks exhausted.

WOLF: Look what she has been doing. What a lovely pattern she has woven with the pine needles.

BEAR CUB: Shhh! Let her sleep. She looks so weary. Let's finish the job for her while she rests.

WOLF: *[As he begins to work]*   A carpet of needles

                                          From the forest pine tree;

                                          We'll weave it together,

                                          Just you and me.

BEAR CUB: We'll weave without stopping

              Until we are done;

              We'll finish before

              The next morning sun.

              [Felicia's music]

              [Curtain]

SCENE 7:	Throne room

[Onstage: King, Queen, Rottina, *and* Pamela; *enter* Prince*]*

PRINCE:	Good morning, everyone.
QUEEN:	Good morning, dear.
KING:	Good morning, Son.
ROTTINA:	Well, it's been three days. I don't see your little forest friend here with the three things your father commanded her to bring.
PAMELA:	Yes, those tasks would be impossible for anyone to complete.
KING:	Has she given up yet, Son?
PRINCE:	I don't think she has given up. She has asked that we meet her in the forest.
QUEEN:	Has she completed her tasks?
PRINCE:	Yes, she says they are complete.
ROTTINA:	Impossible!
PAMELA:	It can't be done!
ROTTINA:	How do you know she has completed them?
PRINCE:	This morning I saw the lock of the great lion's mane and the carpet woven from pine needles.
KING:	But what about the silver?
QUEEN:	Surely you cannot have seen the silver! There isn't....
KING:	Hush, dear. Son, please go on.
PRINCE:	Felicia wished to keep the third part a secret, even from me. That is why she desires us to go to the forest. She wants to show it to us there.
ROTTINA:	Well, I'm not going into the forest! There will be snakes! Ugh!
PAMELA:	And bugs! Ooh!

ROTTINA: Creepy vines!

PAMELA: Wild animals!

ROTTINA: Crawling spiders! *[Exits]*

PAMELA: Hairy monkeys! *[Exits]*

PRINCE: Mother and Father, please come with me.

            [Curtain]

SCENE 8:   Forest with waterfall

            [Onstage: Felicia; *enter* Prince, King, *and* Queen*]*

FELICIA: Good morning, Your Majesty.

KING: Hello, Felicia.

QUEEN: Good morning. Our son tells us you wanted to meet us here. I hope we are not wasting our time.

FELICIA: Thank you for coming here.

KING: Well, let's get on with it.

QUEEN: Do you have anything to show us?

PRINCE: Felicia has three things to show you.

QUEEN: But how?

PRINCE: I know you did not think she could possibly fulfill the tasks you set before her, but her kindness and goodness have worked a kind of magic.

KING: I do not understand.

PRINCE: Watch and see. With gentleness and love she has charmed the creatures of the forest and has earned their trust. The animals are her friends, and the power of their love for her has wrought magic in the forest.

            [Enter Leo*]*

FELICIA: Here is a lock from the mane of the great lion of the forest.

KING: How do we know it is truly from the great lion?

LEO: The great lion is my father. He will be glad to tell you himself that this is from his mane.

FELICIA: Thank you so much, Leo.

LEO: You are welcome. Good-bye, Felicia. *[Exit]*

             [Enter Wolf and Bear Cub]

WOLF: Here is the carpet of pine needles from the forest floor.

BEAR CUB: See how tightly woven it is. And see the pattern the green and brown needles have made.

QUEEN: It is beautiful.

FELICIA: Thank you.

             [Exit Wolf and Bear Cub]

FELICIA: Now I need you to follow me deeper into the forest.

KING: I asked you to show us where to find the silver hidden in the forest. Is this what you intend to do?

FELICIA: Yes.

KING: *[To audience]* I don't know how she can show us what does not exist! Heh, heh!

FELICIA: Look over there.

             [All characters move toward waterfall.]

PRINCE: How beautiful! It is a waterfall!

FELICIA: Look at the water droplets. See how they sparkle and shine.

QUEEN: The drops of water gleam silver and white.

FELICIA: These glittery silver drops of water are more precious than any silver coins. Without this water, we would all die—all of us, the animals, and the very trees of the forest in which we stand.

PRINCE:	How wise! Deep in the forest is the most precious silver of all. Father and Mother, what do you have to say? Has Felicia completed all three tasks?
KING:	It is hard for me to admit, but I was wrong. Felicia, you have revealed great wisdom in showing us these silver droplets.
QUEEN:	And your kindness which has charmed the forest creatures also has won our hearts.
KING:	It was wrong to give you tasks which could not be completed.
QUEEN:	And yet you did complete them.
KING:	You have taught us both a lesson in doing so.
PRINCE:	Then may we marry with your blessing?
KING:	Yes, with our blessing.

[Felicia *and* Prince *embrace.* King *and* Queen *begin to exit.]*

QUEEN:	But who will tell Rottina?
KING:	Not I!
QUEEN:	Surely not I!
KING:	Do not make me do it!
QUEEN:	I will not be the one!

[Exit King *and* Queen; *Enter* Leo, Wolf, *and* Bear Cub]

PRINCE:	You will be my princess, as I knew you should be.
WOLF:	You will live in the castle!
LEO:	Someday you will be queen of the kingdom!
BEAR CUB:	But you will still be our forest princess.
FELICIA:	I will always love my prince, and I will always love you, my forest friends!

[Curtain]

The Land of Rainbows

PUPPET-MAKING NOTES:

Use the directions in chapter 2 for felt hand puppets and figures 2.9 and 2.10 for the basic body and face patterns. A pattern for the rabbit is given in figure 2.12. Facial features for Billy may be taken from figures 2.14 and 2.18. For ideas for Pelly, the pelican, and the Rain Witch, see figure 2.25.

CHARACTERS:

Cotton, the rabbit
Pelly, the pelican
Billy
Rain Witch (dressed in black)
Narrator (any puppet, or a person standing just to the side of the stage, in view of the audience)

SCENERY:

Raindrop Mountains (mostly black and gray)
Rainbow with characters from children's literature, including Winnie the Pooh, Mickey Mouse, Pegasus, and unicorns
Two cardboard flowers, one on either side of the stage, which remain in place throughout the show. May be held by people behind the stage or attached to the stage; must be able to be turned from front to back. Flowers are brightly colored on one side and black on the other. Colorful sides face audience until witch enters in scene 3. Flowers turn to black whenever the witch is onstage and return to colors when she exits.

PROPS:

Small rope for tying up Billy in scene 3
Handkerchief for covering up Billy's mouth in scene 3
Small book

SCENE 1:	Background is blank
	[Onstage: Narrator]
NARRATOR:	This is the story of a young boy named Billy. Listen to what happened to him.
	[Enter Cotton]
COTTON:	Hi, everyone! I've got a problem I need to tell you about.
NARRATOR:	Wait a minute! Who are you?
COTTON:	My name is Cottontail Hopper III, but everyone calls me Cotton. I've been thinking about my friend Billy and how he lost his imagination.

NARRATOR: I was going to tell them about Billy.

COTTON: You? Do you know Billy?

NARRATOR: Well, no, not really.

COTTON: Then let me tell it.

NARRATOR: Oh, OK. *[To audience]* I'll see you later. *[Exit]*

COTTON: Well, as I was saying, my friend Billy lost his imagination. Oh, not all at once. From what I hear, it took a while. Life sure must be dull for Billy now. I just don't know what to do. *[Looks down behind stage]* What's that you say? Oh, OK. *[Looks at audience]* I have another friend named Pelly. I think he wants to come up and see you. Why don't you help me out. On the count of three, everyone say, "Come on out, Pelly." Are you ready? Good. One, two, three: Come on out, Pelly!

   [Enter Pelly]

PELLY: Hi! I'm Pelly the Pelican....

COTTON: They know you're a pelican. They can see that. We need to talk about Billy.

PELLY: Yes, Billy, poor little boy. He used to have so much fun. He used to love painting and drawing.

COTTON: But people told him he was wrong. *[Mimicking]* "Paint the sky blue, Billy, not yellow. Leaves are green, not purple."

PELLY: Pretty soon, Billy stopped drawing at all.

COTTON: Yes, and he used to enjoy reading storybooks where unicorns could dance, and horses could fly, and animals could talk. He wrote a story about a talking cow. But someone told him that cows can't talk. Someone laughed at him. So he stopped reading those books. He started saying, "Animals can't talk, and horses can't fly, and there's no such thing as unicorns."

PELLY: Well, I don't know about the horses and unicorns, but we're talking, aren't we?

COTTON: Yes, we are. That's why I think it's up to us to help Billy.

PELLY: Billy seems to have lost his imagination. I wonder ... do you think we could help him find the Land of Rainbows, where imagination lives?

COTTON: Yes, that's it! The Land of Rainbows! If we can help him find it, he'll see that with just a little imagination, the sky and leaves can be any color at all. Let's go!

[As they walk across the stage, they sing or chant the following:]

PELLY:	We're going to find Billy;
COTTON:	We're going to help him see
PELLY:	That in the Land of Rainbows
COTTON:	Imagination sets you free.
PELLY:	In this land of magic
COTTON:	All the colors shine,
BOTH:	And if you want to make a picture, any color will be fine!

[Curtain]

SCENE 2: Background is blank.

[Onstage: Narrator and Billy; Billy sits with head down.]

NARRATOR: Poor Billy. For several days, he had been bored. He couldn't think of a thing to do. He thought about painting a picture. *[Billy looks up]* But then he remembered that he didn't like to paint any more. *[Billy looks back down]* He thought about reading a book. *[Billy looks up]* But he had decided that made-up stories were a waste of time. *[Billy looks back down]*

[Exit Narrator; Enter Pelly and Cotton as Billy speaks]

BILLY: Horses can't fly, and there's no such thing as unicorns, and animals can't ... talk....

PELLY: Look. There he is.

COTTON: Billy, get up.

PELLY: *[Walking over to Billy]* Young man, you look like a boy who is suffering from imaginitis.

COTTON: *[Walking over and looking closely at Billy]* Pelly, you are absolutely correct. I think this is a severe case of imaginitis.

BILLY: Imagi-- what?

PELLY: Imaginitis. Total loss of imagination.

COTTON: Hmm ... this looks serious. There's only one way to cure this dreadful affliction.

             [Cotton and Pelly walk to one side of stage and whisper to each other. Billy, curious, gets up, moves toward them, and tries to listen.]

PELLY: Oh, ho! So you want to know what to do about it, do you?

BILLY: Y-yes. Can you help me?

COTTON: We can help you only if you really, truly want to be cured.

BILLY: Well ... things were more fun before I got imagi-- imaginitis.

PELLY: Billy, the only way to get your imagination back is to journey with us to the Land of Rainbows.

BILLY: The Land of Rainbows? I never heard of such a place. Are you sure there is such a land?

COTTON: Are we sure? Of course we're sure!

BILLY: Then where is it?

PELLY: um ... er.... *[Loud whisper]* Cotton, where is it?

COTTON: Well, now, let me think for a minute.

BILLY: See, I don't think there is a Land of Rainbows.

COTTON: Wait a minute. *[Exits and returns with a small book]* Here, in this book ... let me see ... Land of Rainbows ... Here it is. *[Reads]* Go north for ten miles. Turn right and head east for five miles. Cross the Spider River. Go over the Raindrop Mountains, and you will find yourself in the Land of Rainbows, where imagination lives. *[Looks up]* See, it's right here in this book.

PELLY: Oh, dear, Cotton. Look what else it says. *[Reading]* This is not an easy journey. The Raindrop Mountains are the most difficult part of the trip. Beware of the Raindrop Witch, who destroys imagination and turns all colors black. *[Looking up]* Oh dear, Cotton, I don't know....

COTTON: Billy, I'm willing to risk even the Raindrop Witch to help you reach the Land of Rainbows, if you really, truly want to go there.

BILLY: How long will it take?

COTTON: Oh, two or three days to reach the Raindrop Mountains, but after that, I don't know.

BILLY: Pelly, will you come, too?

PELLY: Well, uh *[Looks at book and then back at* Billy*]* Oh, all right. If it will help get rid of your imaginitis, OK. I'll go.

COTTON: But, Billy, you really have to believe in the Land of Rainbows. And you will have to be very brave.

BILLY: I know. Please stay with me the whole time. I don't want to be left alone.

PELLY: You can count on us.

[The following is chanted]

COTTON: We're going on a journey;

PELLY: We're going to help Billy see

COTTON: That in the Land of Rainbows

PELLY: Imagination sets you free.

ALL THREE: In this land of magic

All the colors shine,

And if you want to paint a picture

Any color will be fine.

[All exit]

[Curtain]

SCENE 3: Raindrop Mountains

[Onstage: Pelly, Cotton, *and* Billy, *asleep]*

[Flowers turn black as Witch *enters and looks around.]*

WITCH: Ynech, ech, ech!

[Exit Witch. *Flowers turn back to colored side.]*

COTTON: *[Waking up]* Well, another day is about to begin. Pelly, Billy, wake up. It's been three days, and we've made it to the Raindrop Mountains.

BILLY: And just on the other side of the mountains is the Land of Rainbows?

COTTON: That's right.

PELLY: We'll have to move quickly today. We don't want to be in the mountains tonight when it's dark.

BILLY: I'm scared. The mountains are so high, and the sky is so dark up there. And I just know the Raindrop Witch is somewhere out there.

PELLY: Sometimes it helps to think about other things and to talk about them. Let's talk as we walk.

COTTON: Billy, tell us why you've been so sad lately.

BILLY: Well, I once liked to draw and paint and read. And I liked to sing.

    [Witch enters behind other characters, unseen. Flowers turn black. Witch exits, and flowers brighten again.]

PELLY: But what happened?

BILLY: I don't know. I didn't like it when people told me my pictures didn't look right. You know, purple leaves, yellow skies, blue horses, red grass. They looked beautiful to me.

COTTON: They sound beautiful to me, too.

PELLY: You had a wonderful imagination.

BILLY: But I don't any more. I don't even care. People told me I was wrong.

COTTON: The other children?

BILLY: No, it was mostly the grown-ups.

PELLY: Oh, Billy.

COTTON: You weren't wrong. They were. That's why we're on this trip.

BILLY: I'm awfully hungry now. We didn't take any time out for breakfast.

PELLY: *[To* Cotton*]* Do you think we have time?

COTTON: Well, I suppose we should eat, but keep your eyes and ears open. You never know when the Raindrop Witch will turn up.

[Enter Narrator*]*

NARRATOR: As Cotton and Pelly began to prepare breakfast, Billy couldn't resist climbing to the top of a nearby hill.

*[*Billy *moves away from the others.]*

BILLY: Look! From up here, I can see for miles!

NARRATOR: He looked to the left, and he looked to the right.

*[*Witch *enters, sneaking up from behind* Billy. *Flowers turn black.]*

NARRATOR: And he looked straight out in front of him. But there was one place Billy did not look.

*[*Witch *jumps out in front of* Billy. Billy *jumps and screams.]*

WITCH: Ah hah! So you're going to the Land of Rainbows, are you? Heh, heh, heh! You'll never make it over the mountains! Never!

*[*Billy *runs back to* Pelly *and* Cotton.*]*

WITCH: *[Calling]* Never! Heh, heh, heh! *[Exit. Flowers brighten.]*

COTTON: Billy, what's wrong?

BILLY: The, the, the w-w-witch, the witch, the Raindrop Witch!

PELLY: You saw her?

BILLY: Yes, and she said we'll never make it to the Land of Rainbows. Pelly, Cotton, I'm scared!

COTTON: Come on! Let's hurry! The map in the book showed a shortcut over that mountain. No time to eat now. Let's go!

NARRATOR: Cotton, Pelly, and Billy walked and walked all day. They climbed up steep mountains, trying to hurry, but also being careful not to slip. They helped each other up; they helped each other down, over and over, one mountain after another.

[*While* Narrator *speaks,* Billy, Cotton, *and* Pelly *move in an up-and-down motion. Flowers turn black as* Witch *enters and follows at a distance.*]

NARRATOR: Finally it began to grow dark. The darkness scared Billy, Pelly, and even Cotton as it crept all around them. It surrounded them with an eerie silence and made it impossible to see what might lurk ahead.

[*Exit* Witch. *Flowers brighten.*]

BILLY: I don't think I can go on. We haven't eaten a thing all day, and we haven't stopped to rest.

PELLY: You know, Cotton, traveling up these steep mountains in the dark would be dangerous. One slip of the foot, and we could go tumbling off the mountain.

COTTON: We have just one more mountain to climb, if our map is correct. I think we should go on.

PELLY: I guess you're right. We have to stop thinking about how tired we are and about the darkness. We're almost in the Land of Rainbows!

NARRATOR: Cotton and Pelly were so determined to make it out of the Raindrop Mountains that as they hurried, they did not notice that Billy was falling farther and farther behind.

[*Exit* Pelly *and* Cotton*]*

BILLY: I'm … too … tired … to … take … another … step. *[Lies down]*

[*Enter* Witch, *who walks close to* Billy, *looking at him. Flowers turn black.*]

WITCH: *[Quietly, to audience]* Heh-heh! If I can keep him from reaching the Land of Rainbows, he'll never get his imagination back! *[Loudly]* Ha, ha! I've got you now!

BILLY: *[Jumping up]* Help! Cotton, Pelly, help me!

[*Exit* Witch, *dragging* Billy *with her. Flowers remain black. Enter* Cotton *and* Pelly.*]*

COTTON: Billy, Billy, where are you?

PELLY: Billy, can you hear us? Billy! Cotton, what will we do?

COTTON: Pelly, do you have the book?

PELLY: Yes, but this is no time to sit and read.

COTTON: Just give it to me!

PELLY: But what good will it do us now?

COTTON: I have an idea.... I remember reading something ... let me see ... yes, that's what we'll do. But first we have to find Billy and the Witch.

NARRATOR: As the night grew even darker, Cotton and Pelly began to search the area where they had last seen Billy. They peered under rocks, behind trees, and even up into the branches of trees. *[Exit* Narrator*]*

               [Enter Billy *and* Witch, *who remain near side of stage.* Billy *is tied with a rope and has a handkerchief over his mouth.]*

BILLY: *[Muffled]* HELP! HELP!

WITCH: It's no use. They'll never find you now! It's too dark. You'll never get to the Land of Rainbows now. What good is imagination anyway? What good are flying horses, and unicorns, and Mickey Mouse, and Winnie the Pooh? They're not real! They're all a waste of time!

               [At other side of stage, Cotton *and* Pelly *look toward* Billy *and then at each other.]*

COTTON: Shh! Don't let her hear us. OK. You know what you have to do.

               *[*Pelly *goes to the flower closest to him and "picks" it. Puppeteer holds flower in front of* Pelly, *or if the puppet has hands,* Pelly *may hold it.]*

PELLY: Come on! *[Moves toward* Witch *and* Billy, *followed by* Cotton*]*

WITCH: So! You've come to rescue your friend, have you? You'll never save him! He's in my power. He believes that skies are blue and cows are brown, and there's no changing that.

               *[*Pelly *holds up flower with black side toward* Witch.*]*

WITCH: That will do you no good. Only bright colors will destroy the Raindrop Witch.

COTTON: We know that!

[Pelly turns flower so bright side faces Witch.]

WITCH: Oh, no! Get those colors away from me! Get them away from me! Take them away! Away…. *[Witch falls down, motionless.]*

[Cotton frees Billy, and the other flower becomes brightly colored again.]

BILLY: Thank you! Oh, thank you! *[Looks at Witch]* Is she dead?

COTTON: Let's just say she won't bother anyone for a long time.

BILLY: I do believe in the Land of Rainbows, and I do want to get there tonight.

COTTON: Let's go! *[Leads the others offstage, carrying flower in front of him, bright side forward)*

> ALL THREE: We're going on a journey;
> We're going to see
> That in the Land of Rainbows
> Imagination sets us free.
> In this land of magic
> All the colors shine,
> And if we want to paint a picture,
> Any color will be fine!

[Curtain]

SCENE 4: Rainbow with characters

[Enter Cotton, Pelly and Billy]

BILLY: It's beautiful! But I don't understand. It's still night. Yet the sun is shining here.

PELLY: In the Land of Rainbows, anything is possible.

BILLY: Look! Horses can fly! Unicorns do exist!

COTTON: There's Mickey!

PELLY: And Winnie!

BILLY: They're all here! And all the colors of the rainbow, too!

PELLY: Billy, I think your imaginitis is gone.

BILLY: I left it back in the Raindrop Mountains. When I get home, I'm going to draw and paint and read and play.

COTTON: But before we go home, let's explore this wonderful land.

[The following may be sung.]

ALL THREE: In this land of magic

All the colors shine,

And if we want to paint a picture,

Any color will be fine!

[Curtain]

Cousins

PUPPET-MAKING NOTES:
Patterns for puppet body and face are in figures 2.9 and 2.10 in chapter 2. Patterns for facial features may be taken from figures 2.14 and 2.18.

CHARACTERS:
Mom
Amy, eight years old
Dad
Charlie, Amy's brother
Mrs. Clark, Amy's teacher
Lynnette, Amy's eight-year-old cousin

SCENERY:
Amy's house (kitchen)
Amy's classroom

MUSIC:
Ballet music

PROPS:
Photograph
Ballet skirt for Amy
Curly wig for Amy
Lace collar for Amy

SCENE 1:   Amy's house

[Onstage: Amy; *enter* Mom*]*

MOM: Amy! Oh, there you are. I have news for you.

AMY: News?

MOM: I've had a letter from Aunt Kathy. She's agreed to let your cousin, Lynnette, spend a few weeks with us this summer. Won't that be fun?

AMY: I guess so.

MOM: Is that all? Just "I guess so"?

AMY: Well, I haven't seen Lynnette since we were both five years old. That was more than three years ago. I hardly even know her.

MOM: That's why she's coming out here—so you can get to know each other better.

AMY: But what if we don't like each other? What if she wants to leave as soon as she gets here?

MOM: I wouldn't worry about that, Amy. I'm sure you two will get along just fine. Here ... Aunt Kathy sent a photograph so you can see what Lynnette looks like now. *[Shows* Amy *the photograph]*

AMY: She looks pretty.

MOM: Yes, she looks like Aunt Kathy.

AMY: She doesn't look like she'd enjoy herself here.

MOM: Why do you say that?

AMY: Well, she looks so ... so....

MOM: Ladylike?

AMY: Yes. Dainty, sweet.

MOM: Oh, I'm sure she likes to do many of the things you like to do.

AMY: I can't picture her on a skateboard or climbing a tree. She looks as if she likes playing with dolls and going to tea parties. Oh, Mom, this is going to be a terrible summer!

MOM: You're jumping to conclusions, Amy. You don't really know her yet. Why don't you write Lynnette a letter? Tell her what you like to do, and ask what her interests are.

AMY: Well, OK, but I think it will take more than a letter to make this summer a good one.

MOM: I'll get you a piece of stationery so you can get started. *[Exit]*

AMY: OK.

              [Curtain]

SCENE 2:   Amy's house

              [Onstage: Dad; *Enter Amy]*

DAD: Hi, honey bunny.

AMY: Hi, Dad. I was looking for you.

DAD: Oh yeah? What's up?

AMY: Remember the dollhouse you made for me when I was five?

DAD: Of course I remember it. Why?

AMY: Well, I made you put it up in the attic when school started last fall.

DAD: I know. You said you were too big to play with dolls. You were afraid Pam and Jolene and your other friends would laugh if they saw it in your bedroom.

AMY: Yeah, I know. The thing is, Dad....

DAD: What, honey?

AMY: Well, can you bring it back down again?

DAD: Of course I will! Have you decided you're not too old for it after all?

AMY: Not exactly, but I think I may need it this summer.

DAD: OK. I'll bring down the dollhouse later this evening.

AMY: Thanks, Dad.

            [Exit Dad; *Enter* Charlie*]*

CHARLIE: Hi, Amy! Do you want to go out and shoot some baskets?

AMY: Yes. It's nice to know I can be myself around my brother.

CHARLIE: What?

AMY: Never mind. Let's just go play.

CHARLIE: Sometimes you're weird, Amy.

            [Exit Amy *and* Charlie*]*

            [Curtain]

SCENE 3:   Amy's house

[Onstage: Amy *in ballet skirt; Enter* Mom*]*

MOM: Amy, what in the world do you have on?

AMY: It's my ballet skirt, Mom, remember?

MOM: Isn't it a bit small for you? You took ballet two years ago. And you didn't enjoy it.

AMY: I hated it, and, yes, this skirt is small. I can hardly breathe in it!

MOM: Then why....

AMY: I got a letter from Lynnette today. She takes ballet lessons. She'll probably want to practice while she's here. She probably won't have time to do any of the things I like to do.

MOM: Did she say that in her letter?

AMY: Well, no. But I thought I'd better brush up on some of the dance movements and positions.

MOM: Well, all right. But I don't really think that's necessary. Lynnette isn't coming out here to practice ballet all day long. *[Begins to exit]* I'm going next door for a few minutes.

AMY: Good! No one will see me trying to do ballet.

MOM: What?

AMY: Have a good time, Mom. Don't hurry.

[Exit Mom. *Ballet music plays as* Amy *tries to stand on her toes and stumbles.]*

AMY: Oops! Oof!

*[Amy *tries a jump and falls on her face as* Charlie *enters. Stop music.]*

CHARLIE: You sound like a herd of cows and look like a baby trying to take her first steps!

AMY: Charlie, you're mean! No one was supposed to be watching.

CHARLIE:	If I were you, I'd take off that ballet skirt. You look funny.
AMY:	Ooh, Charlie. Just leave me alone! *[Exit]*
CHARLIE:	*[To audience]* I tell you, she's acting strange!
	[Curtain]
SCENE 4:	Amy's house
	[Onstage: Charlie, Mom, Dad*]*
MOM:	Amy is really worried about Lynnette's visit.
DAD:	I know. I've never seen her so worried.
CHARLIE:	It's just a visit from a dumb cousin.
MOM:	Please don't refer to Lynnette as a "dumb cousin."
CHARLIE:	You know what I mean. It's just not something to get all worked up about.
DAD:	Where is Amy, anyway? It's time for dinner.
CHARLIE:	I'll go get her. *[Exit]*
MOM:	In just another week, school will be out, and Lynnette will be here.
	[Enter Charlie*]*
DAD:	Where's Amy?
CHARLIE:	She's locked in the bathroom. She says she'll be here in a minute.
MOM:	Well, let's begin eating before it all gets cold.
CHARLIE:	Broccoli again?
MOM:	It's good for you.
DAD:	I made some of my famous cheese sauce to put on it.
CHARLIE:	Good! If I put on enough sauce, maybe I won't taste the broccoli.

DAD: Well, just leave some for your sister.

                [Enter Amy *in wig and lace collar]*

DAD: Well, well! Who is this? I don't seem to recognize you.

CHARLIE: Ha, ha, ha! Amy, who frizzed your hair? You don't look like you!

MOM: Charlie!

CHARLIE: Well, she doesn't!

DAD: I think you look very pretty with curly hair and all dressed up.

MOM: You just have to learn how to use my curling iron correctly.

DAD: What's the occasion?

AMY: Occasion?

MOM: You really want Lynnette to like you, don't you?

CHARLIE: How can she like something as funny looking as that?

MOM: Charlie!

AMY: I never want to see you again, Charlie Taylor!

                [Amy cries and runs offstage; curtain]

SCENE 5:   Amy's classroom

                [Onstage: Amy *and* Mrs. Clark*]*

MRS. CLARK: Amy, I'd like to see you for a minute before you go home.

AMY: Yes, Mrs. Clark?

MRS. CLARK: I read the paper you wrote about your summer plans. It helped me understand something a little more clearly.

AMY: Oh?

MRS. CLARK: You've seemed unhappy and nervous the past few weeks. And you haven't been acting like the Amy I know.

AMY:	Mrs. Clark, did you ever wish that summer would never arrive?
MRS. CLARK:	I always look forward to summer vacation!
AMY:	I'm not looking forward to this summer.
MRS. CLARK:	When I was eleven years old my family moved to a new town. There was a girl my own age who lived right next door to my new house.
AMY:	Did you become friends?
MRS. CLARK:	Best friends. And it wasn't because we were exactly alike. She played the violin and loved to go fishing with her father. I loved to read, and I couldn't stand to touch a worm or a cold, floppy fish. But we got along just fine.
AMY:	But how do I know that Lynnette and I will get along?
MRS. CLARK:	You don't know for sure that you will. But if you do, it probably won't be because you are exactly the same. Think about what our world would be like if every person was just like everyone else. We all have our own interests and ideas. That's what makes our world so interesting. It's what keeps this world going. You and Lynnette will each have things to teach the other. Perhaps she'll help you gain an interest you never had before. Promise me you'll think about that, OK, Amy?
AMY:	OK, Mrs. Clark. I'll try.
MRS. CLARK:	Remember, the prettiest flower garden is the one with many different kinds of flowers growing in it. Do you know what I mean?
AMY:	I think so. Lynnette may turn out to be a rose, while I am a daisy. But we can both grow in the same garden.
MRS. CLARK:	And your differences will make that garden all the more interesting. Have fun when Lynnette is here. Not everyone is lucky enough to have a cousin her own age.
AMY:	Good-bye, Mrs. Clark.
MRS. CLARK:	Good-bye, my daisy.

[Curtain]

SCENE 6:	Amy's house
	[Onstage: Mom *and* Lynnette*]*
MOM:	Well, Lynnette, you've been here for three days. Are you having fun?
LYNNETTE:	Oh, Aunt Susan, I'm trying to have fun. I really am! I looked forward to coming out here for weeks!
MOM:	But you're not enjoying yourself?
	[Enter Amy*]*
LYNNETTE:	Not really.
AMY:	I knew it, Mom! I knew it! She hates it here! Lynnette, maybe you should just go back home!
LYNNETTE:	Maybe I should!
MOM:	Girls! Girls! Let's talk about this. Calm down right now. *[Pause]* OK, Lynnette, why aren't you enjoying yourself? Can you tell us?
LYNNETTE:	Well, I expected to come out here and have a lot of fun, but Amy is acting really weird.
AMY:	Weird? Weird?
LYNNETTE:	Well, you always want to stay inside and play with your dollhouse or practice ballet.
AMY:	But I thought you liked ballet!
LYNNETTE:	I do like ballet. But I don't want to do it all the time. And I still like to play with dolls, but just every once in a while. There are so many things I was hoping we could do together.
AMY:	Like what?
LYNNETTE:	I brought my skateboard.
AMY:	You did? Do you like to play ball, too?
LYNNETTE:	All kinds of ball—softball, basketball....
AMY:	But you just didn't look like....

LYNNETTE:	Like the kind of girl who likes to do those things? Oh—you're thinking of the photograph my mom sent. It was taken on my birthday, and my mom made me wear a dress for the picture. And I can't do anything about my hair. It's naturally curly!
AMY:	It is?
LYNNETTE:	Yes, and I wish it was straight like yours.
AMY:	Oh boy, have I been acting like a dummy!
MOM:	Amy, I think you forgot what Mrs. Clark told you. And what we've been trying to tell you.
AMY:	Yeah, I guess I did. Lynnette, your middle name isn't Rose by any chance, is it?
LYNNETTE:	Rose? No. Why?
AMY:	Never mind. It's not important. Come on! Let's go get our skateboards!
LYNNETTE:	Oh, Amy? Do you think you could call me Lynn? Lynnette just seems too fancy.
AMY:	OK, Lynn. Let's go!
AMY AND LYNNETTE TOGETHER:	This is going to be a super summer!

[Curtain]

The Smartest Person in the Village

PUPPET-MAKING NOTES:

Felt hand puppets or Styrofoam head puppets may be used. Felt puppet patterns for people are provided in chapter 2, figures 2.9, 2.10, 2.14, and 2.18.

CHARACTERS:

Innkeeper
John, a boy
Judge
Five guests at the inn (may be a mixture of men and women)
Jeanetta, the woman

SCENERY:

The outside of an inn, with a rooster prominently featured.

PROPS:

Black cooking kettle, large enough to be seen easily by the audience. This may be a two-dimensional cardboard kettle, a plastic kettle, or a real pot. It must be black.

Four black patches to apply to the palms of four of the guests to indicate sooty palms. A piece of Velcro in a color matching the hand may be sewn to each hand. The other half of the Velcro will be sewn to the black patch. When the guests bend to touch the kettle, the puppeteers quickly press the patches onto the hands, out of the audience's sight behind the kettle or just below the performance area of the stage.

〰〰〰

SCENE 1:	*[Onstage:* Innkeeper*]*
INNKEEPER:	John! John! Come here at once!
	[Enter John*]*
JOHN:	Yes, sir? Is something wrong?
INNKEEPER:	Yes, John. In all my years of being an innkeeper, I have never been robbed. Never, that is, until this morning.
JOHN:	Someone robbed you?
INNKEEPER:	Yes! A thief has taken all my money. And as you are my helper, you must do something.

JOHN:	What can I do?
INNKEEPER:	First, all of the guests are in the dining room. I suspect that one of them is the robber, as the inn's doors are still locked and no one has entered the inn since yesterday. Bring the suspects to me. Then go into town and fetch the judge. Surely he will be able to settle this.
JOHN:	Yes, sir. I will do as you ask. *[Exit]*
	[Curtain]
SCENE 2:	*[Onstage:* Innkeeper, Judge, five suspects*]*
JUDGE:	*[To* Innkeeper*]* So you believe that one of these people has robbed you?
INNKEEPER:	Yes. One of them has taken all of my money from the cash box.
JUDGE:	Well, let's get started. *[Looks at* Guest #1*]* You, there!
GUEST #1:	M-me?
JUDGE:	Yes, you. Where were you last night and this morning?
GUEST #1:	I passed the night in my room and went directly to the dining room for breakfast this morning.
JUDGE:	And you. *[Looking at* Guest #2*]* I suppose you did the same?
GUEST #2:	Yes, sir, I did. I never left my room last night.
JUDGE:	And you went straight to your room this morning?
GUEST #2:	I give you my word.
GUEST #3:	And I, too, give you my word.
GUEST #4:	I am innocent!
JUDGE:	*[To* Guest #5*]* And what about you?
GUEST #5:	The innkeeper knows me. I have stayed here many times. I have never given him reason to distrust me.
JUDGE:	So you all say you are not thieves.

ALL FIVE GUESTS:	I didn't do it! I'm innocent!
INNKEEPER:	We're not getting anywhere.
JUDGE:	This will require further study.
	[Curtain]
SCENE 3:	*[Onstage:* Innkeeper *and* John*]*
JOHN:	Sir, I have an idea. I have heard that in the very center of the village lives a woman who is the smartest person in the village.
INNKEEPER:	Jeanetta. Yes, I have heard of her. Many tales are told of her cleverness.
JOHN:	I will bring her to you at once.
INNKEEPER:	And I will call the suspects back again.
JOHN:	*[As he exits]* I hope we have better luck this time.
	[Enter the five guests]
GUEST #1:	Why must we stay here?
GUEST #2:	Yeah, we want to be on our way!
GUEST #3:	This is silly.
GUEST #4:	I already told you, I didn't do it!
GUEST #5:	Oh, let's get this over with and hear what he has to say.
INNKEEPER:	Thank you.
	[Enter Jeanetta*]*
JEANETTA:	What's the trouble? What's the trouble? Always there's trouble. Do I know you?
INNKEEPER:	This morning someone robbed me of all my money. These five guests were the only people in the inn, and I think it was one of them.
GUEST #1:	We have already been questioned by a judge.

JEANETTA: Oh, I don't think I need to question you.

GUEST #2:   Good! Then we may go?

JEANETTA: Not so fast! *[To* Innkeeper*]* Fetch me the iron cooking kettle.

INNKEEPER: The iron pot? But it is so old and blackened by soot. How will this help?

JEANETTA: You will see. Just bring the kettle, and turn it upside down.

INNKEEPER: As you wish.

              [Curtain]

SCENE 4:   *[Onstage:* Innkeeper, Jeanetta, *and the five guests; kettle is center stage, upside down.]*

JEANETTA: Now we are ready.

GUEST #3:   What good will a dirty old pot do?

JEANETTA: Silence! Listen to me. Each of you must place a hand on the kettle. *[Points to rooster]* When the guilty person touches the pot, that rooster will crow three times.

GUEST #4:   What can a dumb, old rooster tell you?

JEANETTA: Hush! It is the kettle that will tell us who is guilty.

GUEST #5:   The kettle?

JEANETTA: Now! One by one, touch the kettle.

              [Each guest touches the kettle with one hand by placing a hand behind the pot. As this is done, a black patch is pressed onto the hand of each guest except Guest #3. This must be done out of sight of the audience.]

INNKEEPER: The rooster did not crow.

GUEST #2:   We told you we were innocent!

GUEST #4:   What a waste of time.

              [All guests laugh]

JEANETTA: Not so fast! Let me see your hands.

[Guests hold up their hands so their palms are visible to the audience.]

JEANETTA: *[Pointing to Guest #3]* You! You are the guilty one!

GUEST #3:   No! No!

JEANETTA: Oh, yes! You are guilty.

INNKEEPER: But how do you know?

GUESTS #1
AND #5:   Yes, how do you know?

JEANETTA: That one knew he was guilty, so he did not dare touch the kettle. He did not want the rooster to crow when he touched it.

INNKEEPER: You truly are the smartest person in the village. Thank you! Thank you, Jeanetta!

JEANETTA: The kettle never lies!

[Curtain]

Selected Bibliography

Adair, Margaret Weeks. *Do-It-in-a-Day Puppets for Beginners*. New York: John Day, 1964.

Buchwald, Claire. *The Puppet Book: How to Make and Operate Puppets and Stage a Puppet Play*. Boston: Plays, 1990.

Champlin, Connie, and Nancy Renfro. *Storytelling with Puppets*. Chicago: American Library Association, 1985.

Creegan, George. *Sir George's Book of Hand Puppetry*. Chicago: Follett, 1966.

Currell, David. *The Complete Book of Puppet Theatre*. Totowa, N.J.: Barnes & Noble, 1987.

Engler, Larry, and Carol Fijan. *Making Puppets Come Alive: A Method of Teaching and Learning Hand Puppetry*. New York: Taplinger, 1973.

Flower, Cedric, and Alan Fortney. *Puppets, Methods and Materials*. Worcester, Mass.: Davis, 1983.

Fraser, Peter. *Introducing Puppetry*. New York: Watson-Guptill, 1968.

Hanford, Robert Ten Eyck. *The Complete Book of Puppets and Puppeteering*. New York: Sterling, 1976.

Hawes, Bill. *The Puppet Book*. San Diego, Calif.: Beta Books, 1977.

Marks, Burton, and Rita Marks. *Puppet Plays and Puppet-Making*. Boston: Plays, 1982.

Mulholland, John. *Practical Puppetry*. New York: Arco, 1961.

Philpott, A. R., ed. *Eight Plays for Hand Puppets*. Boston: Plays, 1968.

Renfro, Nancy. *A Puppet Corner in Every Library*. Austin, Tex.: Nancy Renfro Studios, 1978.

Robson, Denny. *Puppets*. New York: Gloucester Press, 1991.

Ross, Laura. *Puppet Shows Using Poems and Stories*. New York: Lothrop, Lee & Shepard, 1970.

Tichenor, Tom. *Tom Tichenor's Puppets*. Nashville: Abingdon Press, 1971.

Yerian, Cameron, and Margaret Yerian, eds. *Puppets & Shadow Plays*. Chicago: Children's Press, 1974.

Index

About the Author

Toni A. Schramm is a school librarian at Hawthorn School in Vernon Hills, Illinois, and a summer puppet workshop leader at Lake Villa District Library in Lake Villa, Illnois. She has taught both high school English and elementary language arts. She was named to Who's Who in American Colleges and Universities in 1972-73, and graduated summa cum laude from California Lutheran University in 1974 where she won the Mark van Doren Memorial Poetry Prize awarded by the university. She earned her M.A. in teaching at Northwestern University in 1975.